ESSENTIAL HISTORIES

Russia's Wars in Chechnya 1994–2009

Mark Galeotti

OSPREY PUBLISHING
Bloomsbury Publishing Plc
Kemp House, Chawley Park, Cumnor Hill, Oxford OX2 9PH, UK
29 Earlsfort Terrace, Dublin 2, Ireland
1385 Broadway, 5th Floor, New York, NY 10018, USA
E-mail: info@ospreypublishing.com
www.ospreypublishing.com

OSPREY is a trademark of Osprey Publishing Ltd

First published in Great Britain in 2024

The text in this edition is revised and updated from: ESS 78: *Russia's Wars in Chechnya 1994–2009* (Osprey Publishing, 2014).

Essential Histories Series Editor: Professor Robert O'Neill

A catalogue record for this book is available from the British Library.

ISBN: PB 9781472858221;
eBook 9781472858214;
ePDF 9781472858252;
XML 9781472858245;
Audio 9781472858238

24 25 26 27 28   10 9 8 7 6 5 4 3 2 1

Cover design by Stewart Larking
Maps by Peter Bull Art Studio, revised by www.bounford.com
Index by Zoe Ross
Typeset by PDQ Digital Media Solutions, Bungay, UK
Printed and bound in India by Replika Press Private Ltd.

Osprey Publishing supports the Woodland Trust, the UK's leading woodland conservation charity.

To find out more about our authors and books visit www.ospreypublishing.com. Here you will find extracts, author interviews, details of forthcoming events and the option to sign up for our newsletter.

CONTENTS

INTRODUCTION

A bullet, a bomb, or a missile cannot, will not, destroy us.
This will not end. We will sooner or later revenge ourselves
upon you for the deeds you have done to us.
– Open letter from the 'Wolves of Islam' movement to
the people of Russia, 1995

Post-Soviet Russia fought its first war – the First Chechen War – in 1994–96. In effect, it lost: a nation with a population of 147 million was forced to recognize the effective autonomy of Chechnya, a country one-hundredth its size and with less than one-hundredth of its people. A mix of brilliant guerrilla warfare and ruthless terrorism was able to humble Russia's decaying remnants of the Soviet war machine.

But this was a struggle that had already run for centuries, and was not going to end there, not least as Moscow feared that, as a multi-ethnic land empire, where Chechnya went, others might follow. Russia licked its wounds and built up its forces for a rematch, invading again in 1999 and by 2009 declaring the Second Chechen War won. However, this did not mean peace in Chechnya, where the organised guerrilla movement may well have been suppressed at the time of writing, but sporadic terrorism continues against the ruthless local regime. Nor did it bring true peace to the wider North Caucasus region, which was infected by insurrection and continues periodically to experience outbreaks of violence. It is also worth questioning just how much of a victory this really was for Moscow, given that its price has been installing Ramzan Kadyrov, an erratic warlord-turned-president who in many ways runs Chechnya as his own private kingdom, as well as having to provide massive amounts of federal funding to rebuild the country and buy off Kadyrov and his allies.

OPPOSITE

A Chechen rebel, an Islamic green band sewn onto his hat as a recognition symbol (given his Soviet-era army coat), with a slung PKM machine gun. (Photo by David Brauchli/Sygma via Getty Images)

The beautiful but often unforgiving terrain of Chechnya is evident from this gorge outside Grozny. (Abdullah Bersaev / EyeEm / Getty Images)

If only Boris Yeltsin, first president of post-Soviet Russia, had been more aware of his own country's history. After all, it is hardly surprising that the first and most serious direct challenge to Moscow's rule after the collapse of the USSR came from the Chechens. An ethnic group from the North Caucasus mountain region on Russia's southern flank, the Chechens – who call themselves *Nokhchy* or *Vainakh* – have lived in the region for thousands of years, their land defined by the Sunja and Terek rivers to the north and the west, the Andi mountains to the east and the mighty Caucasus range to the south. Their reputation has been as a proud, fractious, raiding people. This is, after all, a land of mountains and valleys. Diagonal ranges cut the country from north-west to south-east, with the lowland valleys and hillsides in between often thickly forested. This is perfect bandit and guerrilla country, but also a geography that worked against the rise of any strong central power.

Instead, what emerged was a people divided but united, politically divided between clan (*teip*) and family, but with a shared culture characterized by a close-knit sense of community, based on tradition, kinship and a fierce sense of honour, valuing independence to an immense degree. The Russians came to realize this when their own imperial expansion brought them to the North Caucasus in the 18th century, their eyes fixed on other prizes: Georgia to the south, and beyond that, Safavid Iran and the Ottoman Empire. Of all the North Caucasian mountain peoples, the Chechens put up the fiercest resistance to the Tsarist Russian invaders of the 18th and 19th century and Soviet occupiers of the 20th. They would suffer the most for it, too, including massacres and forced deportations. Leaders such as Sheikh Mansur and, especially, Imam Shamil (ironically, an Avar from present-day Dagestan, not a Chechen) have become symbols of national pride and independence alongside modern-day figures such as former elected Chechen president and tactical genius Aslan Maskhadov, the man who masterminded the counter-attack that saw Russian forces pushed out of the Chechen capital, Grozny. A bandit tradition, of the so-called *abreg* or *abrek* – a wronged man who strikes back against abusive lords, like a Robin Hood of the North Caucasus – has metamorphosed into the cult of the guerrilla. A generation of Chechens reached adulthood having known nothing but conflict and the messy, brutal counter-insurgency operations which followed the formal end of the war in 2009, and the repressive, personalistic Kadyrov regime. That regime, built on subsidies from Moscow, thuggish authoritarianism and the whims and vanity projects of its leader, has rebuilt Grozny as a glittering capital, yet allowed many Chechens to continue to live in poverty. It has also assumed an outsized role in Russian politics and, indeed, around the world. Kadyrov's assassins have gone after critics of the regime not just within Russia but across Europe. Meanwhile, Moscow has found itself unable to curb him or even stop funding this notoriously corrupt regime, as Kadyrov in effect blackmails the Kremlin by threatening to step down. Given that the assumption – rightly or wrongly – is that without him and his army of oath-sworn fighters (the so-called '*Kadyrovtsy*'), Chechnya might descend into chaos, triggering a Third Chechen War, Moscow has to date backed down every time.

After all, the conflict proved pivotal in shaping post-Soviet Russia, too. The First Chechen War demonstrated the limits of the new democracy. Although Yeltsin had originally told the constituent republics and regions of the Russian Federation to 'take as much sovereignty as you can stomach', when the Chechens took him at his word, he proved too much of a nationalist to be willing to see his country break apart. It also undermined his credibility with the military and the country alike, forcing him to fall back on questionable political alliances and outright vote-rigging to hold on to power. On the other hand, the second war was the making of the hitherto-unknown prime minister and then president Vladimir Putin, allowing him to present himself as the saviour of Russian territorial integrity, the scourge of terrorists and kidnappers and the strong man able to succeed where Yeltsin had failed.

The Chechen wars of 1994–96 and 1999–2009 were dramatic, vicious and complex affairs, full of extremes of heroism, atrocity and unexpected reversals. An irregular guerrilla force proved able to drive a modern army out of Grozny, for example, when well motivated and brilliantly led. Conversely, the Russians demonstrated an impressive ability to learn from their mistakes when they subsequently created a Chechen force of their own, able to take the war to the rebels on their own terms. As such, the Chechen wars covered the whole spectrum of modern conflict, from a handful of relatively conventional clashes between regular units, through hard-fought urban battles to the bitter military and political campaigns of terrorism and counter-insurgency. In many ways they epitomized a new paradigm of war, as armies come to terms with warfare that is more often asymmetric and political, as much about winning hearts and minds – or at least shattering the enemy's will to fight – as carrying the day on the battlefield.

These wars would even reverberate into Russia's other colonial conflicts. Many ethnic Chechens who lived over the border in the Pankisi Gorge region of Georgia supported the rebels. This became a lasting source of friction between Tbilisi and Moscow – only a small part, but a part nonetheless, of the reason why Russian so forcibly supported break-away regions of Georgia and invaded in 2008. Chechen loyalists were deployed to bolster separatist forces in Ukraine's Donbas region from 2014, while others joined Ukrainian government militias. After the full-scale Russian invasion of 2022, Kadyrov's men served alongside other Russian forces, while four 'battalions' – closer to companies in actual strength – of volunteers joined Kyiv's defenders (see pp. 133–34). As one retired Russian army officer who had served in the Second Chechen War told the author in 2019, 'we are fooling ourselves if we think that war ended anything. It was just another skirmish in a war that will only end when the Chechens are free.' He then added, 'and Russia is free of them.'

A Chechen volunteer armed with an AK-74 takes cover behind a rebel tank during street fighting in Grozny on 1 January 1995, during the initial Russian assault. (Photo by OLEG NIKISHIN/AFP via Getty Images)

BACKGROUND TO WAR
Home of the wolf

We are free and equal, like wolves.
– Chechen saying

Homeland of the wolf

The national symbol of the Chechens, visible everywhere from badges and knife pommels to the flag of the independent 'Chechen Republic of Ichkeria' – Ichkeria is the traditional Turkic name for the region – is the wolf, *borz* in Nokhchy, which is also the name of their language. Chechen folklore stresses the wolf's role as both loner and pack-member and this duality is visible in Chechen society, too. It is traditionally dominated by the tribe and the clan (*teip*), each being made up of lines (*gars*) and families (*nekye*), governed by the male elders who interpret the *adat*, traditional law. While the *adat* and the collective wisdom of the elders are important, though, these are forever in tension with an egalitarian, competitive and aggressive spirit of adventure and independence.

To the Chechens, after all, the wolf symbolizes courage and a love of freedom, but also implicitly a predator's spirit. Traditionally, Chechen culture was a raiding one, in which young men would prove themselves by raiding other tribes and *teips* – even ones with whom they were

Rebel warlord Ruslan Gelayev giving a press conference in front of a rebel flag in Urus-Martan in October 1995. A relatively effective communicator, as well as commander, he would go on to become a deputy prime minister under Maskhadov. (ALEXANDER NEMENOV/AFP via Getty Images)

on good terms – for horses or cattle or even brides. These raids, which were meant to be essentially bloodless (although a raider caught by his intended victims might face a good beating before being released or ransomed), were also ways of maintaining the skills that would make the Chechens formidable guerrillas. Killing another Chechen would simply bring blood feud from his kin; the feud is a powerful force in such a society, and in some cases ran from generation to generation.

Historically the Chechens have thus been politically fragmented but culturally united. While sharing the same language, identity and traditions, individual tribes and *teips* essentially managed their own affairs, except when some common enemy threatened. Then they would typically unite behind some charismatic warlord, such as Imam Shamil in the 19th century and Dzhokhar Dudayev in the 21st, to break apart once again when the conflict was over or the leader had fallen.

Chechens meet Russians

The only good Chechen is a dead Chechen.
– Attributed to General Alexei Yermolov, 1812

Traditionally, Russian attitudes towards the Chechens have been complex, a mix of fear, hatred and respect. In the main, the Russians have considered the *gortsy*, the 'mountaineers' as they sometimes call the peoples of the North Caucasus, to be generally untrustworthy, wily yet primitive. However, the Chechens assumed a special place in the 19th-century Russian idea of the Caucasus, sometimes the noble savage, often just the savage. Mikhail Lermontov's *Cossack Lullaby*, for example, includes the lines, 'The Terek runs over its rocky bed./ And splashes its dark wave;/A sly brigand crawls along the bank;/Sharpening his dagger', while in the song the Cossack mother reassures her child that 'your father is an old warrior; hardened in battle'. There was something different, something alarming about the Chechens. To a considerable extent this reflects the tenacity, skill and ferocity with which they have fought against Russian imperialism since the earliest contacts.

Although Cossack communities, seeking an independent life outside Tsarist control, settled in the North Caucasus as far back as the 16th century, it was really only in the 18th century that the Chechens and the Russian state encountered each other. There were skirmishes during Peter the Great's 1722–23 Caucasus campaign against Safavid Iran that showed that the Chechens in their home forests were not to be taken lightly, but it was the struggle against Sheikh Mansur (1732–94) which began in 1784 that truly alerted the Russians to the threat they faced. A Chechen Muslim *imam*, or religious leader, educated in the Sufi tradition, Mansur was angered by the survival of so many pre-Islamic traditions within Chechnya and campaigned for the universal adoption of *sharia* Islamic law over the *adat*. He declared a holy war – *jihad* or, in the North Caucasus, *gazavat* – initially against 'corrupt Muslims' who did not recognize the primary of *sharia* and, coincidentally, his own authority.

This was an essentially domestic issue, but Mansur's message became increasingly popular across the North Caucasus as a whole and followers of other ethnic groups began flocking to his cause. When the Russian

A portrait of Tsar Peter the Great from the collection of the State Central Artillery Museum. It was during the reign of Peter I that Russians first began to tangle with Chechens. (Photo by Fine Art Images/ Heritage Images/ Getty Images)

authorities heard that he was planning to invade neighbouring Kabardia to spread his word, and even opening negotiations with the Ottoman Empire, they became alarmed. The Ottomans were the Russians' main rivals along their south-western flank, and Mansur's holy war could easily and quickly be turned against Orthodox Christian Russia. Contemptuous of Mansur's 'scoundrels' and 'ragamuffins', the Russians sent the Astrakhan Regiment into Chechnya, to Mansur's home village of Aldy. Finding it empty, they put it to the torch, handing Mansur perfect grounds to declare *gazavat* against the Russians. Ambushed by the Chechens at the Sunzha River crossing as they marched back, the Russians were massacred: up to 600 were killed, 100 captured and the regiment disintegrated, individuals and small groups hunted down as they tried to flee through the woods.

Buoyed by this success, Mansur gathered a force of up to 12,000 fighters from across the North Caucasus, although Chechens were the largest contingent. His skills were as charismatic leader rather than strategist, though, and Mansur made the mistake of crossing into Russian territory and trying to take the fortress of Kizlyar. Fighting the Russian Army on its own terms and in its own territory, Mansur's forces were routed. Although Mansur would remain active until his capture in 1791, whenever he took the field against the Russians, he lost. Even so, he had demonstrated that the Chechens could be formidable when united against a foreign enemy and fighting their own kind of war.

Hitherto, though, Chechnya had been considered something of an irrelevance, a land rich only in troublesome locals. The real prize was Georgia to the south, and the real enemies were Safavid Iran and the Ottomans. When Georgia was annexed in 1801, secure routes to Imperial Russia's newest possession began to matter. Once Russia found itself at war with both Iran (1804–13) and the Ottoman Empire (1807–09), the need to shore up the Caucasus flank meant that St Petersburg finally decided it was time to extend its rule in the North Caucasus.

The chosen instrument was General Alexei Yermolov, an artilleryman who had distinguished himself during the war with Napoleon and who was made viceroy of the Caucasus. He set out to subjugate the highlands by a policy of deliberate, methodical brutality. His strategy was to build fortified bases and settlements across the region, to bring in Cossack soldier-settlers and to respond to risings and provocations with savage reprisals. Infamously, he affirmed, 'I desire that the terror of my name shall guard our frontiers more potently than chains or fortresses.'

Yermolov was especially wary of the Chechens, whom he considered 'a bold and dangerous people'. He founded the fortress of Grozny in 1818 – the name means 'Dread' – as a base from which to control the central lowlands. His aim was to pen the Chechens in the mountains, clearing the fertile lowlands between the Terek and

The uncompromising nature of General Yermolov, commander of Russian forces in the Caucasus, is evident in this portrait. (Art Collection 3 / Alamy Stock Photo)

Sunzha rivers for Cossack settlers. They in turn would cut down the forests that gave the Chechens such an advantage. In 1821, the Chechens held a gathering of the *teips* to unite against the Russians; Yermolov responded with a campaign to drive the Chechens into the highlands with fire, shot and sword. Even so, the Chechens were beleaguered but not beaten. In a sign of things to come,

Iman Shamil remains a folk hero and nationalist icon in Chechnya, even though he ended up a captive of the Russians, as shown in this photograph. (Photo by Fine Art Images/Heritage Images/Getty Images)

terrorism and assassination began to supplement raids in their tactical repertoire. In 1825 two of Yermolov's most notorious officers, Lieutenant-General Dmitri Lissanievich and Major-General Nikolai Grekov, died when an imam, brought in for interrogation, produced a hidden dagger and stabbed them both. The Russians executed 300 Chechens in reprisal.

In 1827, Yermolov was recalled and removed, the victim of court politics rather than as a result of any discomfort about his methods. His successors followed broadly similar policies, albeit with less ruthless enthusiasm. However, the next phase of the Russo-Chechen conflict would instead be initiated and defined by the 'mountaineers', specifically Imam Shamil (1797–1871), a Dagestani who raised the North Caucasus in rebellion and who remains a cultural hero for the Chechens to this day.

Shamil was a fighter as well as a religious figure, the de facto moral leader of the scattered 'mountaineer' resistance movement from 1834. At first, he tried to come to terms with the Russians, offering to accept their sovereignty and end raids on the lowlands, in return for a degree of cultural and legal autonomy. Major-General Grigory Rosen – who in 1832 had led a force of almost 20,000 troops across Chechnya, systematically burning crops and villages – rejected any thought of compromise. In part, this was precisely because the Russians feared the Chechens. In 1832, one officer admitted that 'amidst their forests and mountains, no troops in the world could afford to despise them' as they were 'good shots, fiercely brave [and] intelligent in military affairs'. Lieutenant-General Alexei Vel'yaminov, Yermolov's chief of staff, noted that they were 'very superior in many ways both to our regular cavalry and the Cossacks. They are all but born on horseback.'

The Russians, thinking themselves on the verge of victory, simply increased the pressure. In 1839, Shamil only barely managed to escape when besieged for 80 days at Akhoulgo. The Russians took some 3,000 casualties before eventually storming this fortified village. However, they overplayed their hand and tried to implement a range of policies, meant to quash Chechen spirits once and for all. *Pristavy*, government inspectors recruited from local collaborators, were given wider powers, which they typically used to persecute and plunder. Lowland Chechens were forbidden to have any contact with their upland relatives – or even sell them grain, one of their main sources of income. Then the Russians tried to disarm the Chechens, confiscating weapons which were seen as the main accoutrements of manhood and were often cherished family heirlooms. However, all this served only to rekindle the rising.

Shamil combined Mansur's charisma with rather greater military acumen. He raised the North Caucasus in a rebellion characterized by guerrilla attacks rather than set-piece battles in which Tsarist discipline and firepower could prevail. In 1841, General Yevgeni Golovin – who had previously quelled a Polish uprising – warned that the Russians had 'never had in the Caucasus an enemy so savage and dangerous as Shamil'. Ultimately, though, he would fail. It was perhaps inevitable when set against the whole weight of the Russian Empire. After the end of the Crimean War in 1856, the Russians were able to deploy fully 200,000 troops to the Caucasus. In 1859, Chechnya was formally annexed to the Russian Empire and Shamil was captured, whereupon he was treated as an honoured prisoner. He was brought to St Petersburg for an audience with Tsar Alexander II before being placed in luxurious detention first in Kaluga and then Kiev. In 1869 he was even permitted to make the hajj pilgrimage to Mecca and he died in Medina in 1871. In an irony of history, while two of his four sons continued to fight in the Caucasus, the other two would become officers in the Russian military.

Soviet Chechnya

The backward Dagestani and Chechen masses have been freed from the cabal of the White Guard officer class and the lies and deceptions of parasitic sheikhs and mullahs.
– Bolshevik statement, 1921

The Chechens were not to be pacified for long, and generation after generation rose against Russian rule, only to be beaten back down. Despite initial hopes that the collapse of the Russian Empire in 1917 and subsequent

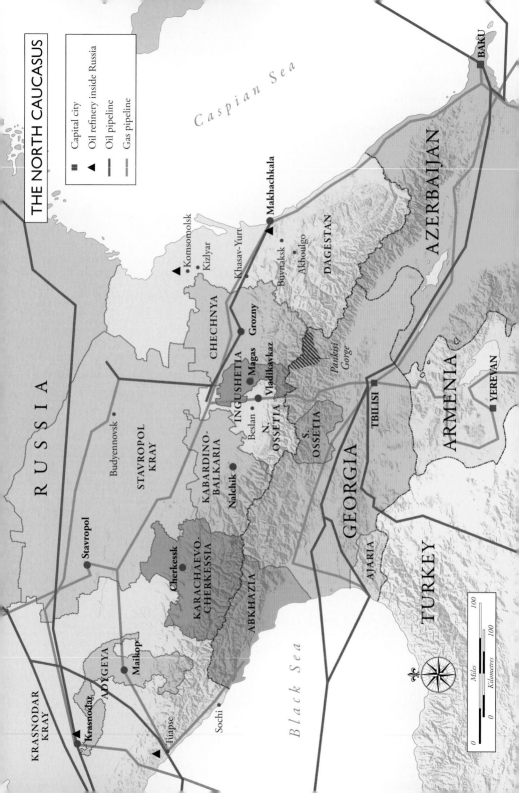

THE NORTH CAUCASUS

Capital city
Oil refinery inside Russia
Oil pipeline
Gas pipeline

Caspian Sea

BAKU

Black Sea

RUSSIA

KRASNODAR
KRAY

Krasnodar

Tuapse

Sochi

ADYGEYA

Maikop

Stavropol

Budyennovsk

STAVROPOL
KRAY

Cherkessk

KARACHAEVO-
CHERKESSIA

ABKHAZIA

KABARDINO-
BALKARIA

Nalchik

Komsomolsk

Kizlyar

Khasav-Yurt

CHECHNYA

Grozny

Magas

INGUSHETIA

Beslan

N.
OSSETIA

Vladikavkaz

S.
OSSETIA

Pankisi
Gorge

Makhachkala

Buynaksk

Akhoulgo

DAGESTAN

AZERBAIJAN

GEORGIA

TBILISI

AJARIA

TURKEY

ARMENIA

YEREVAN

Miles   100
Kilometres 100
0

Bolshevik take-over would mean their freedom, the Chechens found that the Soviets simply followed in their imperial predecessors' footsteps. A Union of the Peoples of the North Caucasus was founded in 1917 and formally declared the independence of the region in 1918. During the Russian Civil War (1918–22), they found themselves clashing with White – anti-Bolshevik – forces under General Anton Denikin. The Whites were pushed out of the Caucasus in 1920 largely by Chechen and other forces – Denikin himself called the area a 'seething volcano' – and when they arrived, the Bolsheviks were greeted as liberators. However, nationality policy and the Caucasus campaign lay in the hands of an ambitious and uncompromising Bolshevik by the name of Joseph Stalin. He was not inclined to dismantle Russia's empire and in 1921, the Mountaineer Autonomous Soviet Socialist Republic (Gorsky ASSR) was established, subordinated to Moscow. Already, though, Russian insensitivity and Bolshevik attempts to supplant Islam had triggered a new rebellion, which lasted for around a year. Over time there were various territorial reorganizations – in 1924, the ASSR was divided into various districts and regions – but in essence, one imperial master had been replaced by another.

In the name of administrative efficiency and state control, in 1934 Stalin – now General Secretary and unquestioned ruler of the USSR – arbitrarily merged the Chechen and Ingush Autonomous Regions into one. The Chechens rebelled again and again were crushed. However, Stalin never forgot a slight. In 1944, concerned that the Chechens might again rise while the Soviets were locked in conflict with Nazi Germany, he decided on a characteristically dramatic solution. Near enough over a single fateful night, 23 February, the entire Chechen population of 480,000 was deported in Operation *Chechevitsa* (Lentil). Up to 200,000 died in what the Chechens often describe as the *Ardakh*, the Exodus. Resettled and scattered across Central Asia, Siberia and Kazakhstan, the Chechens were only allowed to return to their homeland in 1956, after Stalin's death. Even then, this tragedy remained under a veil: only in the 1990s was a memorial to the victims raised in central Grozny, bearing the inscription, 'We will not break, we will not weep, we will never forget.' (Controversially, it was dug up and moved to a less visible location in 2008.)

There would be no more risings, but Mikhail Gorbachev's liberalizing reforms in the 1980s allowed the Chechens to campaign for the freedom they had so long been denied. A nationalist movement known as the Chechen All-National Congress rose to prominence, led by a mercurial and charismatic former air-force general, Dzhokhar Dudayev (1944–96). Ironically it was a last-ditch effort by hard-liners to preserve the USSR, the three-day 'August Coup' in 1991, which finally shattered the Union and gave Dudayev his chance. He used the opportunity to overthrow the existing Soviet administration in Grozny, declare independence and call for elections in October, which he duly won. This was largely overlooked in those final tumultuous months of the USSR, but when Gorbachev dissolved the Soviet state at the end of the year, Chechnya became newly independent Russia's problem. While the Chechens had been a thorn in Gorbachev's side, Russian leader Boris Yeltsin tolerated them. But once Dudayev began advocating secession from his new Russian Federation, Yeltsin had no more time for him. Yeltsin declared the election null and void and issued a warrant for Dudayev's arrest, sending a battalion of MVD VV (Ministry of Internal Affairs Interior Troops) in a failed bid to enforce it. This proved the true catalyst of Chechen nationhood. The more Moscow inveighed against Dudayev, the more he became canonized as a hero of national independence. While still legally part of Russia, Chechnya became effectively independent. In December 1992, Ingushetia formally broke away to become a republic on its own within the Russian Federation, while Chechnya increasingly challenged Moscow. Dudayev believed, it appears, that this time the Russians would be unable or unwilling to spend blood and treasure bringing the Chechens back into the fold. He was wrong.

WARRING SIDES
Soldiers versus fighters

Russian troops, when confronted with heavy armed and determined Chechens, have simply stood aside – something I saw with my own eyes.
– Journalist Anatol Lieven, *Chechnya: tombstone of Russian power* (1998)

Just as in conflicts past, this would be an asymmetric conflict from the first – although the Russians would eventually learn a hard-fought lesson, that the best way to fight a Chechen is with another Chechen. In the main, though, the two Russo-Chechen wars saw a conventional military machine and a nimble local insurgent movement each seeking to force the other to fight on their terms.

Russian and federal forces

Moscow certainly had all the advantages on paper. At the time of their first invasion, at the end of 1994, the Russian Armed Forces officially numbered over 2 million, on paper. However, this was a war machine whose gears were rusty, whose levers were broken and whose fuel was sorely lacking. It was really just an exhausted fragment of the old Soviet Armed Forces, unreformed and largely unfunded: it was receiving only 30–40 per cent of the budget it needed simply to maintain its fighting

Russian soldiers ride a BTR-60 personnel carrier as they move through Grozny in 1995. The 'Soldier of Fortune' markings are strictly unofficial, and reflect the shaky state of discipline at the time. (ALEXANDER NEMENOV/AFP via Getty Images)

condition, let alone modernize and reform. Every unit was actually under-strength. The cohesion of units was often appallingly bad: there was no professional NCO corps to speak of – sergeants were conscripts with a few months' extra training and junior officers performed many of the roles carried out by NCOs in Western armies – and morale was generally poor. After all, pay was low and often late (as of mid-1996, pay arrears had reached $889 million) and even basics such as food and heating in winter were never guaranteed. In a vicious circle, this contributed to a brutal and sometimes lethal culture of hazing and bullying called *dedovshchina* ('grandfatherism') which undermined the interpersonal ties within units so vital in a guerrilla war.

The bulk of federal forces in the Joint Group of Forces (OGV), especially in the First Chechen War, were standard motor-rifle infantry, mechanized infantry in Western parlance. They moved in trucks sometimes, but otherwise BTR-70 and BTR-80 wheeled armoured personnel carriers or BMP-2 infantry combat vehicles, and their units were leavened with T-72 or T-80 tanks. Already rather dated, these tanks were poorly suited for operations in cities and highlands, especially as the reactive armour which might have helped defeat the simple, shoulder-fired anti-tank weapons wielded by the Chechens was available but generally not fitted. Units would cycle in and out of the OGV over the course of the conflicts, but for most of the time they comprised conscripts from the units of the North Caucasus Military District (SKVO), serving two-year terms, whose training – like their equipment – was still essentially based on Soviet patterns. As such, they were geared towards fighting mechanized mass wars on the plains of Europe or China. The painfully won lessons of Afghanistan had often been deliberately forgotten or ignored by a high command that thought it would never again be fighting a similar war. Likewise, the last specialized urban-warfare unit in the Russian military had actually been disbanded in February 1994. Furthermore, units were often cobbled together from elements drawn from other parent structures, without having had time to train together and cohere. As a result, the Russian infantry was largely unprepared for the kind of scrappy yet often high-intensity fighting it would face in Chechnya, lacked effective low-level command and initiative and was often forced to improvise or fall back on raw firepower to make up for other lacks, a factor that contributed to civilian casualties and the federal military's poor reputation with the civilian population.

All that being said, the federal forces should not be considered entirely or uniformly degraded. Some of the units deployed were of distinctly higher calibre, especially the *Spetsnaz* ('Special Designation') commandos and the VDV (Airborne Assault Forces) troops, as well as particular elements of the Russian Armed Forces and the MVD VV (Ministry of Internal Affairs Interior Troops). Indeed, once the qualitative weaknesses of the federal armed forces became clear, there was something of a scrabble to find better-trained and -motivated forces to deploy there, including Naval Infantry marines and

Russian *Spetsnaz* in Khankala being briefed before a mission in May 1995. They are all armed with suppressed assault rifles or, in the case of the man second on the left, a VSS-1 silenced sniper's rifle. (ALEXANDER NEMENOV/AFP via Getty Images)

OMON (Special Purpose Mobile Unit) police riot troops (who were at least professionals, and who were well prepared for urban operations).

Much of the equipment with which the Russians fought had serious limitations or was ill-suited to this conflict. Nevertheless, there were also elements of the Russian arsenal which certainly carried their weight. The Mi-24 'Hind' helicopter gunship, while a design dating back to the late 1960s, nonetheless would demonstrate its value in scouring the lowlands and hillsides alike, just as it had in Afghanistan, especially in the Second Chechen War. By the same token the Su-25 'Frogfoot' ground-attack aircraft proved a powerful weapon in blasting city blocks with rockets and bombs, even though ten were lost through the two wars to enemy fire and mechanical problems. However, much of the key fighting was against snipers and ambushers, and weapons able to bring overwhelming firepower rapidly to bear in these conditions were often crucial. For example, the man-portable RPO-A *Shmel* incendiary-rocket launcher

was often called 'pocket artillery' for its ability to blast a target with a thermobaric explosion equivalent to a 152mm artillery round.

Beyond this, the Russians learned and improvised. When it became clear that their armoured personnel carriers were all too vulnerable to Chechen rocket-propelled grenades, they began welding cages of wire mesh around them to help defeat the enemy's shaped charges. Likewise, the ZSU-23-4 and 5K22 Tunguska self-propelled air-defence vehicles, armed with quad 23mm and double 30mm rapid-fire cannon respectively, were pressed into service as gun trucks; they could elevate their weapons high enough to sweep a hilltop or building roof and lay down withering fire. The acute lack of decent maps of Chechnya, a serious problem in the early days of the invasion, was partly remedied by scouring the closed-down bookshops of Grozny.

It is also important to note that there was a distinct difference between the federal forces that fought in the First Chechen War of 1994–96 and those of the Second, 1999–2009. By 1999 the military and political leadership had learnt many of the lessons of their initial humiliation. They had spent time and money preparing for the rematch and assembled forces that were far more suited to this conflict. Much more and better use was made both of special forces and MVD VV units. The latter are essentially light infantry, although some units are mechanized, with a particular internal-security and public-order role. As a result, they were more prepared for operations in Chechnya, especially those involving mass sweeps of villages hunting for rebels, arms caches and sympathizers. The MVD also disposes of a range of elite forces, from the OMON police units through to its own *Spetsnaz* units, many of which were rotated through Chechnya. Alongside them were deployed a larger number of other elite security forces, including the Alpha anti-terrorist commando unit of the Federal Security Service (FSB).

More generally, the Second Chechen War also saw a greater use of new weapons and equipment, from body armour and night-vision systems for the soldiers to reconnaissance drones in the skies. However, the main changes were in the preparations made beforehand, a willingness to adapt to Chechen tactics – such as by creating special 'storm detachments' for urban warfare – and a more sophisticated overall strategy. If in the First Chechen War the implicit assumption was that Chechens were all threats to be neutralized, in the Second the Russians adopted a two-pronged approach. On the one hand, they were ruthless in their control of the Chechen population, but on the other, they eagerly recruited Chechens, including rebel defectors, to a range of security units, realizing that such fighters were often best suited to taking the war to the rebels. The Russians, after all, had the firepower, but their Chechen allies could often best guide them how and where to apply it.

Chechen forces

Although the Chechen Republic of Ichkeria (ChRI) formally had its own security structures, they did not last long once the war began and the fight was soon in the hands of more irregular units, even if at times they were able to display unusually high levels of discipline and co-ordination. When the Russians invaded in 1994, they faced a Chechen Army, a National Guard and the Ministry of Internal Affairs (Russian bombers had essentially destroyed the Chechen air force on the ground on the eve of invasion). These forces were at once more and less formidable than they seemed: less formidable in that many of the units were far smaller than their titles suggested. The Army, for example, fielded a 'motor rifle brigade' that was actually little more than a company, with some 200 soldiers; the Shali Tank Regiment (some 200 men, with 15 combat-capable tanks, largely T-72s); the 'Commando Brigade' (a light motorized force of 300 men); and an artillery regiment (200 men, with around 30 light and medium artillery pieces). To these 900 or so troops could be added the 'Ministry of Internal Affairs

Regiment', another light motorized force of 200 men. However, about two-thirds of the ChRI's field strength of 3,000 had been drawn from the so-called National Guard. This was a random collection of units, ranging from the gunmen of certain clans through to the personal retinues of particularly charismatic leaders as well as Dudayev's own guard. These had such picturesque names as the 'Abkhaz Battalion' and the 'Muslim Hunter Regiment', few of which truly reflected their real size or role.

However, this ramshackle assemblage of forces did have several significant examples. They knew the country well and while they were no longer quite the hardy outdoorsmen of the 19th century, having adapted to the age of the car, central heating and college, their traditions did grant them a certain *esprit de corps*. They also knew their enemy, most having served their time in the Soviet or Russian military. Indeed, given the martial reputation and enthusiasm of the Chechens, a disproportionate number had served in the VDV or *Spetsnaz*, experience

A Chechen soldier loads his RPG anti-tank grenade launcher as his unit prepares to try to hold the road to Grozny during the initial Russian advance. (MICHAEL EVSTAFIEV/AFP via Getty Images)

Chechen fighters during the Russian occupation of Grozny in 1994. (Photo by Georges DeKeerle/Sygma via Getty Images)

which would serve them well in the coming wars. In age, they spanned the full range from adolescents to pensioners, although the typical fighter was in his mid to late twenties.

While some units still retained a more formal structure modelled on the Russian forces, in the main they fought in units of around 25 men broken into three or four squads. They were largely armed only with light personal and support weapons, especially AK-74 rifles, RPG-7 anti-tank grenade launchers, disposable RPG-18 rocket launchers, SVD sniper rifles, grenades and machine guns. However, thanks to that martial tradition, as well as the preceding years of rampant criminality which had seen guns smuggled into the country and state arsenals opened, they had plenty of those, not least the ammunition and spares the lack of which is often the guerrilla's bane.

Besides which, their numbers would quickly be swollen by volunteers from across the country, from the

A defiant Aslan Maskhadov surrounded by supporters and bodyguards in front of the OSCE security mission office in Grozny in 1995. (ALEXANDER NEMENOV/AFP via Getty Images)

Chechen diaspora elsewhere in Russia and, eventually and ultimately counter-productively, from Islamist militants from the Middle East. This would be an 'army' of warlords and their followings, even if during the First Chechen War and the early years of the Second there was still some sense of a command structure, largely anchored around the person of Aslan Maskhadov (1951–2005), the chief of staff of the Chechen military and later their elected president. Even so, this was a force whose size fluctuated by the season and the day, not least as individuals might take up arms for a particular operation and then return to their civilian activities until the next.

Above all, they were characterized by a fierce determination and excellent tactics. These were often unconventional, but rooted in an understanding of how their enemies operated. Knowing the Russian propensity for the artillery barrage, for example, in urban warfare they 'hugged' Russian units, keeping within a city block or so of them so that the Chechen forces were safe from bombardments. Likewise, the Chechens were well aware that the guns of Russian tanks could not depress enough to engage basement positions, in which they built makeshift bunkers from which to attack Russian advances. Finally, they drew on their strengths, from sticking to using Nokhchy for their communications, knowing the Russians could intercept their radio traffic but not generally understand it, to drawing the federal forces into traps and ambushes in the cities and mountains that they knew so much better.

OUTBREAK
Flashpoint: 1994

Intervention by force is impermissible and must not be done. Were we to apply pressure by force against Chechnya, this would rouse the whole Caucasus, there would be such a commotion, there would be such blood that nobody would ever forgive us.
– President Yeltsin, 10 August 1994

As the USSR began to break apart under General Secretary Mikhail Gorbachev, an opportunist Communist Party boss called Boris Yeltsin (1931–2007), angered by the political machinations that had seen him sacked from his position as First Secretary of Moscow, turned to anti-communist rhetoric to win himself a new political constituency. He won election after election, in July 1991 becoming president of the Russian republic within the USSR. The failed August Coup later that year by hard-line communists opposed even to Gorbachev's more moderate reforms allowed Yeltsin to become the standard-bearer of change. When Yeltsin refused to sign his proposed new Union Treaty, which would have introduced dramatic changes but preserved the USSR, Gorbachev was forced to bow to the inevitable. On the last day of 1991, he signed the USSR out of existence, creating 15 new states, including the Russian Federation.

However, this was a new nation created by default and from the first would encounter challenges between the centralizing impulses of Moscow and the national aspirations of some of the members of this federation. Originally, Yeltsin had suggested that constituent members of the Russian Federation would be free to chart their own destinies, but as ever this proved a promise easier to make while seeking office than to keep once in power. The head of the Chechen-Ingush Autonomous Soviet Socialist Republic, Doku Zavgayev, had failed to repudiate the August Coup and had been hounded out of office. In October 1991, a referendum was held to confirm Dzhokhar Dudayev, then the head of the informal opposition All-National Congress of the Chechen People, as president. He immediately declared the republic independent – something the minority Ingushetians questioned and Yeltsin flatly refused to accept. Moscow declared a state of emergency and dispatched an MVD VV regiment to Grozny. However, when the lightly armed security troops touched down at Khankala airbase outside the city, they were surrounded by a far greater number of Dudayev's forces. Gorbachev refused to let the Soviet Armed Forces get involved and Yeltsin shied away at the time from escalating, so after some tense negotiations the MVD VV troops were allowed to leave by bus. Moscow had challenged Grozny and Grozny had won, the first round at least, leaving Dudayev a national hero and Chechnya believing itself finally free.

In March 1992, a new Federation Treaty was signed as the foundational document of the Russian state and Chechnya refused to take part. As a result, in June Ingushetia formally split from Chechnya, petitioning successfully to be incorporated into the Russian Federation as the Republic of Ingushetia. Meanwhile, the self-proclaimed Chechen Republic of Ichkeria (ChRI) affirmed its own statehood, with a flag and national anthem – even if no international recognition.

This was not a tenable state of affairs. On the one hand, Yeltsin was becoming increasingly worried about

Dzhokhar Dudayev

Born in 1944, Dzhokhar Musayevich Dudayev had experienced Stalin's resettlement at first hand, spending his first 13 years in internal exile in Kazakhstan. Even so, he joined the Soviet Air Force, becoming a bomber pilot in the Long-Range Aviation service. He was decorated for his service during the Soviet–Afghan War in 1986–87, and in 1987 became a major-general, the first Chechen to reach general rank in the air force. He was appointed commander of the 326th Heavy Bomber Division in Tartu, Estonia. This was a nuclear strike force, suggesting that the authorities considered his loyalty beyond question. Nevertheless, while there he seems to have been affected by the growing nationalist mood of the Estonian people and he demonstrated considerable sympathy towards them.

In 1990, when his unit was withdrawn from Estonia, he retired from the military and returned to Chechnya. There he threw himself into nationalist politics and was elected chair of the All-National Congress of the Chechen People. He demonstrated a willingness to take full advantage of circumstances, and when

Dzhokhar Dudayev poses in front of a Chechen flag. A successful Soviet air force commander, he never managed truly to develop a vision for an independent Chechnya. (Photo by Antoine GYORI/Sygma via Getty Images)

local Communist Party boss Zavgayev's position looked shaky after the 1991 August Coup, Dudayev dispatched militants to seize the local parliament and TV station and, in effect, stage a coup of their own, retrospectively legalized in a referendum.

In power, though, Dudayev proved much less effective, largely delegating matters of state to cronies more interested in enriching themselves, while he spent his time practising karate (he was a black belt). When the Chechen parliament tried to stage a vote of no confidence in his leadership in 1993, he had it dissolved. When the Russians invaded in 1995, he continued to lead the government in principle, although operational command soon devolved to more capable field officers. He was killed outside the village of Gekhi Chu on 21 April 1996, while on a satellite phone to a liberal Russian parliamentarian. Although conspiracy theories abound as to booby traps, it seems most likely that he was killed by two missiles fired from a Su-25 attack jet after a Russian electronic intelligence aircraft detected the signal.

the long-term implications of allowing Chechnya's withdrawal from the federation as a precedent. Indeed, Dudayev was eager to create a federation of the Caucasian *gorsky* peoples in the mould of Imam Shamil, although his Confederation of Caucasian Mountain Peoples never amounted to much. The much larger and economically important Republic of Tatarstan had already negotiated for itself special membership terms and there were even fears that territories east of the Urals might seek to break free some day.

Not that the ChRI was stable in any sense. While three of Chechnya's 18 constituent regions were threatening secession, Dudayev began to talk of the forced reincorporation of Ingushetia. Conversely, the Terek Cossack Host laid claim to parts of Chechnya. There appeared ample scope for unrest, local insurrection, even civil war, given that under Dudayev, Chechnya was becoming a virtual bandit kingdom. Organized crime flourished, not least within the new ChRI state apparatus. The Chechen State Bank, for example, was used to defraud its Russian counterpart of up to $700 million using fake proof of fund documents.

Russian oil pipelines which ran through Chechnya were not only at risk of destruction but also being tapped illegally and even though Grozny was still a hub for oil refining, in the first two years of independence not a single new school or hospital was built and industrial production fell – largely as a result of under-investment – by 60 per cent.

Chechnya was becoming a genuine threat. At least as important, Yeltsin needed to prove that no one could challenge Moscow with impunity. There was also a political dimension: increasingly unpopular at home as the economy collapsed, he wanted an enemy and a success to distract the public. A conflict became increasingly inevitable. In August Yeltsin was still describing a military intervention by federal forces as 'impermissible' and 'absolutely impossible'; it was not that he was ruling out action, just that he hoped to rely instead on Chechens opposed to Dudayev, who had formed the Provisional Chechen Council. In October and November 1994, Provisional Chechen Council forces, armed and encouraged by Moscow (and supported by Russian airpower) launched abortive incursions into Chechnya. This proved a disaster; they were easily defeated by Dudayev loyalists, who captured Russian soldiers among them and paraded them on TV. To an extent, this reflected the unexpected level of support Dudayev's regime still had, but it was also a product of poor planning on the Russian side. The Provisional Chechen Council was essentially a tool of Russia's domestic security agency, then still called the Federal Counter-Intelligence Service (FSK), but later the Federal Security Service (FSB). It was the FSK that was pushing for intervention and the troops involved, while drawn from Armed Forces units, had actually been hired by the FSK without the explicit clearance of the Armed Forces High Command. According to the testimony of captured soldiers, FSK recruiters had offered them the equivalent of a year's pay to prepare tanks for the operation, and the same again to crew them in support of the Chechen irregulars. They had

Russian-backed Chechens opposed to Dudayev gathering at Bratskoye on the Russo-Chechen border in November 1994. The soldier on the right appears, by his beret, to be a former Naval Infantryman. (IVAN SHLAMOV/AFP via Getty Images)

also been told that Dudayev had already fled, his forces were demoralized and the people of Grozny were ready to welcome them with flowers and cheers. Instead, of the 78 Russian soldiers accompanying the irregulars into Chechnya in November, only 26 made it home, with the rest killed or captured. When Major-General Boris Polyakov, commander of the elite 4th Guards 'Kantemir' Tank Division, heard that some of his soldiers had been hired by the FSK without his knowledge, he angrily resigned his position.

A handful of
Chechens protesting
in Pushkin Square
in the centre
of Moscow on
12 December 1994,
opposing Boris
Yeltsin and the
intervention into
Chechnya. (YURI
GRIPAS/AFP via
Getty Images)

Russia's Chechen 'Bay of Pigs' put Yeltsin in a position in which he could either escalate or back down. Characteristically, he decided to escalate, encouraged by his compliant defence minister, General Pavel Grachev, who airily reassured him that 'I would solve the whole problem with an airborne regiment in two hours.' On 28 November, a secret session of select members of the Security Council met to consider next steps and decided to invade. This

was then put to the full Security Council the next day, but with Yeltsin and his closest allies set on intervention, there was no real scope for debate, even though Yevgeny Primakov, head of the Foreign Intelligence Service and a veteran Middle East specialist, counselled caution. As a result, on 30 November, Yeltsin signed Presidential Decree No. 2137, 'On steps to re-establish constitutional law and order in the territory of the Chechen Republic'.

THE FIRST INVASION

RUSSIA

Achikulak •

Kochubey •

DAGESTAN

STAVROPOL

Staryy River

Peryomayskoye •

Kizlyar •

Mozdok •

Kamyshev •

CHECHNYA

Dubovskaya •
Kargalinskaya •

④

Novyy Terek River

Naurskaya •

Kalinovskaya •

① Nadterechnaya •

Terek River

Chervlennaya •

Malgobek •

Goragorsky •

② Dolinsky •

Tolstoy-Yurt •

INGUSHETIA

Satsita •

GROZNY

Gudermes •

Nazran •

Sunzha River

③

Argun •

Kadi-Yurt •

Assinovskaya •

Khankala airbase

Beslan •

MAGAS
Ali-Yurt •

Alkhan-Kala •

Alkhan-Yurt •

Shali •

Nozhay-Yurt •

Khasav-Yurt •

Vladikavkaz •

Bamut •

Gekhi-Chu •

Urus-Martan •
Komsomolskoye •

Novye Atagi •

Zandak •

Khatuni •

Kirovauya •

Vedeno •

Argun River

Shatoy •
Sovetskoye •

Botlikh •

C A U C A S U S

Sulak River

M O U N T A I N S

DAGESTAN

GEORGIA

Federal forces

① Bombing raids

② Mozdok Contingent

③ Vladikavkaz Contingent

④ Kizlyar Contingent

0 —— Miles —— 25

0 —— Kilometres —— 25

Even ahead of that vote, on 28 November the Russian air force bombed Chechnya's small air force on the ground and closed its two airfields by cratering the runways. Meanwhile, an invasion force was mustered in three contingents. The first, based in Mozdok, North Ossetia and commanded by Lieutenant-General Vladimir Chilindin, numbered 6,500 men. It was based on elements of the 131st Independent Motor Rifle Brigade, nine MVD VV battalions and the 22nd Independent Spetsnaz Brigade. The second, mustering at Vladikavkaz, North Ossetia, was under Lieutenant-General Chindarov – the deputy head of the Airborne Forces – and comprised 4,000 troops from the 19th Motor Rifle Division and the 76th Airborne Division, as well as five MVD VV battalions. The third, under Lieutenant-General Lev Rokhlin, assembled at Kizlyar, Dagestan, with 4,000 troops drawn from the 20th Motor Rifle Division and six MVD VV battalions. Together with other forces, including the air assets committed to the operation, the total force was around 23,700 men, including 80 tanks, under the overall command of Colonel-General Alexei Mityukhin, commander of the North Caucasus Military District (SKVO).

On 11 December, as Yeltsin disappeared from public view reportedly for a minor operation – to avoid embarrassing questions – federal forces moved into Chechnya along three axes that then split into six. Already that represented a deviation from the original plan, which had envisaged starting on 7 December, but the forces had not been ready. Within three days they were meant to be ready to storm Grozny, but in fact local resistance, bad weather and a rash of mechanical difficulties meant they were not emplaced around the city until 26 December. Nevertheless, they had reached the Chechen capital and the real war was about to begin. When the Russians moved in on 31 December, they were met not by cheering crowds throwing flowers and kisses at their liberators, but by a population mobilized for war and charged by a 200-year history of struggle.

THE FIGHTING
Two wars

A few days are enough to ignite a military conflict; to purge and achieve order [takes] years.
– Commentary in newspaper *Izvestiya*, 1995

Karl Marx had it that history repeated itself, the first time as tragedy, the second time as farce. In this case, while it is hard to deny that the First Chechen War was a tragedy, the Second Chechen War was far from a farce. Instead, it proved that despite all its serious limitations, from a dearth of well-trained troops to a lack of an urban warfare and counter-insurgency doctrine, under Putin the Russian state was nevertheless able and willing to spend resources and political capital to crush this, the most serious Chechen attempt to date to throw off foreign domination. In many ways, then, the two wars stand as stark symbols of the respective unfocused amateurism of the Yeltsin regime and the ruthless determination evident under Putin.

The first battle for Grozny
The Russians' assumption was that seizing Grozny would mean the end of the war. This planning decision showed not only that they had forgotten the experiences of past wars with the Chechens, or even the Soviet invasion of

Afghanistan in 1979; it also drove them to try to push towards and into the city more quickly than they should. Federal forces were gathered in a special Joint Grouping of Forces (OGV) that was predominantly made up of units from the Armed Forces and the MVD, but also included FSB units (including some Border Troops, subordinated to the FSB), elements of the separate Railway Troops and detachments from the Ministry of Emergency Situations (MChS). Co-ordination between these various forces was inevitably going to be problematic, especially as the preparations had been hurried, and this was another factor behind the relatively simple 'drive to Grozny'.

The plan was that these taskforces would push directly to Grozny and surround it. While MVD troops locked down the countryside, Armed Forces units would assault the city from north and south, seizing key locations such as the Presidential Palace, main railway station and police headquarters before the Chechens had had the chance to prepare proper defences, and then mop up any remnants

Russian T-72 tanks, one fitted with a mine-clearing plough, halt near Samashky on the western approaches to Grozny, during the initial encirclement of the city in December 1994. (IVAN SHLAMOV/AFP via Getty Images)

of Chechen resistance as remained. However, the plan ran into problems from the first. The three taskforces – which had had to advance along multiple routes because of the geography and the width and quality of roads – all failed to keep to schedule, so Grozny was never effectively blockaded, especially to the south, allowing its defenders to be reinforced with volunteers and raising their numbers to perhaps 9,000 by the height of the battle. With the Russian first wave only numbering some 6,000 men, given the advantages for the defence in urban warfare, this was a serious development for the federal forces. They were to have to throw substantially more into the fray before they eventually took the city and levelled much of it in the process.

The Chechens had also had longer than anticipated to prepare. Under military chief of staff Aslan Maskhadov, the Chechens established three concentric defensive rings and had turned much of the centre of the city into a nest of ad hoc fortifications. Buildings were sandbagged and reinforced to provide firing positions, while – knowing the Russian propensity for the direct attack – the few tanks and artillery pieces the Chechens had were emplaced to command those roads wide enough for an armoured assault, notably Ordzhonikidze Avenue, Victory Avenue and Pervomayskoye Avenue. Further out, there were defensive positions at choke-points such as the bridges across the Sunzha River, as well as around Minutka Square south of the centre.

The Russian plan called for assault elements of the 81st and 255th Motor Rifle regiments to attack from the north under Lieutenant-General Konstantin Pulikovsky, supported by the 131st Independent Motor Rifle Brigade and 8th Motor Rifle Regiment. Meanwhile, elements from the 19th Motor Rifle Division under Major-General Ivan Babichev would move in from the west, along the railway tracks to seize the central station and then advance on the Presidential Palace from the south. From the east, Major-General Nikolai Staskov would lead assault units from the 129th Motor Rifle Regiment and a battalion of the 98th Airborne Division

OGV commanders in the First Chechen War

1994–95	Colonel-General Alexei Mityukhin (Armed Forces)
1995	General Anatoly Kulikov (MVD)
1995	Lieutenant-General Anatoly Shkirko (MVD)
1996	Lieutenant-General Vyacheslav Tikhomirov (Armed Forces)
1996	Lieutenant-General Vladimir Shamanov (Armed Forces)

again along the railway line to Lenin Square and thence capture the bridges across the Sunzha River. From the north-east, elements of the 255th and 33rd Motor Rifle regiments and 74th Independent Motor Rifle Brigade under Lieutenant-General Rokhlin would take the central hospital complex, from where they could support other advances.

Finally, units from the 76th and 106th Airborne divisions would be deployed to prevent the rebels from firing the Lenin and Sheripov oil-processing factories or chemical works, as well as blocking efforts by the rebels to attack the assault units from behind.

The attack began on 31 December after a preparatory air and artillery bombardment and soon ran into trouble as Chechen resistance proved fiercer than anticipated. The western advance soon bogged down in fierce street-to-street fighting. The eastern group was forced to detour and found itself in a kill-zone of minefields and strong-points. The northern group managed to push as far as the Presidential Palace, but there likewise found itself unable to break dogged resistance, and dangerously exposed by the failure of the other groups. Furthermore, a lack of training, the use of forces cobbled together from elements from different units, and poor morale quickly proved problematic. Advances became snarled in traffic jams of armoured vehicles, friendly fire incidents proliferated and units coming under fire showed a propensity to halt and take cover, rather than press on as intended.

Perhaps the most striking reversal was the fate of the 1st Battalion of the 131st Independent Motor Rifle

Much of the defence of Grozny was improvised: here, Chechen volunteers carry crates of Molotov cocktails into the centre of the city, in preparation for the Russian attack. (OLEG NIKISHIN/ AFP via Getty Images)

Brigade, which by the afternoon of the first day had reached the main railway station and had assembled at the square outside it. There they were ambushed by well-positioned Chechen forces in buildings all around the square, which soon became an inferno of small-arms and RPG fire. When survivors fled into the station building, it was set on fire. When other elements of the 131st tried to support their comrades, they were ambushed and blocked. The battalion lost more than half its men and almost all its vehicles; in effect, it had ceased to exist.

By 3 January, the Russian attack had effectively been beaten back. Their only forces still in the city in good order were Rokhlin's group, which had not been expected to drive to the Presidential Palace and had thus avoided the worst of the fighting and had been able to dig in. Even so, this could only be a temporary respite. The Russians redoubled their air and artillery campaign against Grozny, and adopted a much more cautious campaign, slowly grinding their way through the city. On 19 January, they seized the Presidential Palace – or what was left of it after it was hit by bunker-busting bombs – and although fighting would continue in the south of the city for weeks to come (and Dudayev only left on 8 February), Grozny had essentially fallen. But it was a ruin, strewn with the bodies of thousands of its citizens – estimates range up to 35,000 – in a bloodbath that the Organization for Security and Co-operation in Europe (OSCE) would describe as an 'unimaginable catastrophe'. This would not, however, be the last battle for this ill-fated city.

Yeltsin's messy war

On 6 January 1995, the Security Council had announced that military actions in Chechnya would soon be coming to an end; it was take almost another two weeks before they even controlled the ruins of the Presidential Palace. Contrary to Russian expectations, though, the fall of Grozny did not end the war. Instead, what would follow would devolve into a messy series of local brawls, sieges, raids and feints. The towns of Shali, Gudermes and Argun held out for months, even when bombed with cluster munitions, and federal forces seemed to show little enthusiasm to engage in further urban warfare. Besides which, efforts to take the fight to the rebels outside the towns were continuing to lead to embarrassing reversals. On 31 December, for example, commandos from the 22nd *Spetsnaz* Brigade's 230th Detachment had flown out of Mozdok on three Mi-8MT assault helicopters escorted by two Mi-24 gunships and were landed near the village of Komsomolskoye. However, they were detected by rebels, who began gathering forces for an attack, even as more *Spetsnaz* arrived as reinforcements. The detachment's commander, Major Igor Morozov, who was also the brigade intelligence chief, requested evacuation but no helicopters were available. Encircled by some 200 rebels, in thick fog which made any helicopter sorties to rescue or support them impossible, on 7 January the *Spetsnaz* surrendered: of the 50 commandos, two had died in earlier firefights and 48 were captured, representing the largest haul of *Spetsnaz* prisoners of either war.

Russian Interior Troops *Spetsnaz* patrol the airport in Beslan, North Ossetia, wearing the balaclavas affected by many Russian special forces. (MICHAEL EVSTAFIEV/AFP via Getty Images)

The litany of such incidents, and the continued failure to take and pacify Chechnya's cities, became an increasing embarrassment.

In what became a traditional way of expressing disapproval of the progress being made, Yeltsin decided to change commanders and on 26 January, Deputy Interior Minister General Anatoly Kulikov, head of the MVD VV, was given overall charge of the operation. At the same time, efforts were being made to negotiate a settlement and on 20 February, Maskhadov met his Russian counterpart, Chief of the General Staff General Anatoly Kvashnin. But there was no real scope for agreement: the Russians would accept nothing short of complete capitulation. From the Russians' point of view, at least the pause gave them a chance to regroup and reinforce. More and better troops were rushed to Chechnya, from wherever they could be found: part of the MVD VV's 1st Independent Special Designation Division – the elite 'Dzerzhinsky Division' from Moscow – as well as the

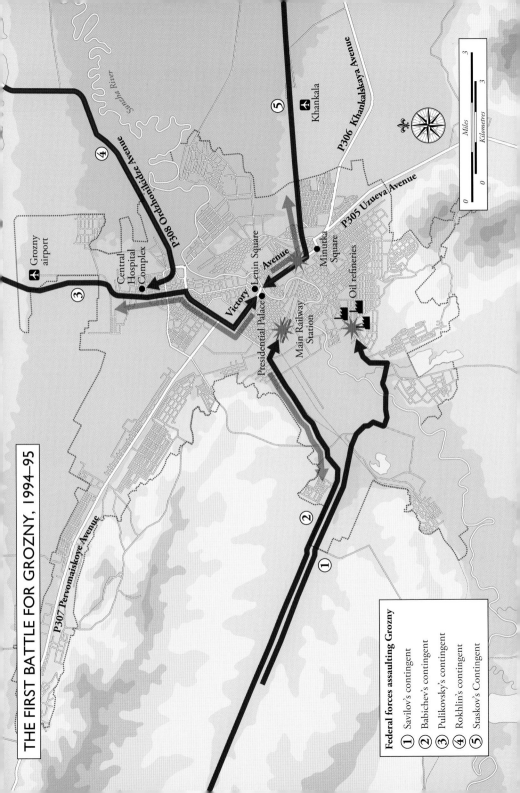

THE FIRST BATTLE FOR GROZNY, 1994–95

Sunzha River

Grozny airport

Central Hospital Complex

P308 Ordzhonikidze Avenue

Khankala

P306 Khankalskaya Avenue

P305 Uzueva Avenue

Victory Avenue

Lenin Square

Minutka Square

Presidential Palace

Main Railway Station

Oil refineries

P307 Pervomaiskoye Avenue

0   Miles   3
0   Kilometres   3

Federal forces assaulting Grozny

1. Savilov's contingent
2. Babichev's contingent
3. Pulikovsky's contingent
4. Rokhlin's contingent
5. Staskov's Contingent

Vityaz anti-terrorist commando unit, Naval Infantry from the Northern, Pacific and Baltic Fleets (though the commander of one Pacific Fleet battalion refused his orders) and the Armed Forces' elite 506th Motor Rifle Regiment. In total, the OGV was brought to 55,000 personnel from the MVD and military. The FSK set up a Chechnya directorate. In short, having realized that this was hardly going to be the quick or neat operation it had anticipated, Moscow hurriedly looked to raise its game.

Ceasefire talks broke down on 4 March; the next day, federal forces began their assault on Gudermes, although this would prove a lengthy, on-and-off process. Argun fell more easily, on 23 March, and by the end of April, most main centres were loosely in federal hands, even if attacks continued regularly. Having originally suggested that Grozny was returning to normal, in May the Russians were forced to introduce a curfew and admitted that hundreds of rebel fighters remained within the city. Colonel-General Mikhail Yegorov, the temporary acting field commander of the OGV, spoke of 20 per cent of the country still being in rebel hands, in the southern highlands around Shatoy and Vedeno – they themselves claimed almost twice that.

Nevertheless, the Russian offensive ground on, with Kulikov asserting that no more than 3,000 fighters still supported Dudayev, a figure that remained suspiciously constant throughout the war (especially as the Russians claimed to kill 17,000 rebels in the course of the conflict). Slowly, the Russians were adapting to the war, learning to coordinate air and artillery fires with their ground attacks more effectively. Vedeno fell on 3 June, and on 13 June, the Russians claimed – and the Chechens admitted – that they had taken Shatoy and the nearby town of Nozhay-Yurt. Moscow began to believe that the end of the war was close.

However, the Russians' notion that this was a conflict whose progress could be charted by map was flawed. Although the rebels only controlled a small portion of southern Chechnya, the Russians had neither the numerical nor the moral strength to be said to control the rest. By day, the Armed Forces and MVD patrolled the cities while Mi-24 helicopter gunships tracked along roads and pipelines and engaged in 'free hunts' across rebel-held areas, engaging at will with guns and rocket pods. There were sporadic bomb and sniper attacks in the cities and ambushes outside, but in the main the Russians did not try to penetrate too deeply into the highlands and villages and the Chechens knew that a direct confrontation with the federal forces would bring a devastating response. By night, though, the Russians largely withdrew to their bases, mounting only occasional and heavy patrols in main cities, abandoning the country to the rebels, who used these times to regroup and relocate. This allowed the rebels to be able to mount attacks throughout the country still. Besides, what was looming was the start of a whole new type of war, one for which the Russians were distinctly unprepared.

War by terrorism

Even as the Russians were making their grandiose assertions, a convoy of trucks was travelling up the P263 highway, into Stavropol Region. Some 195 Chechen fighters under rebel commander Shamil Basayev bluffed and bribed their way past successive police checkpoints, pretending to be carrying the coffins of dead soldiers home. Basayev had hoped to get further into Russia, but on 14 June, they reached a roadblock just north of the southern Russian city of Budyonnovsk 70 miles (110km) north of the Chechen border. Basayev had spent $9,000 in bribes and had run out of money, so instead his party turned round and drove back into Budyonnovsk. They seized the mayor's office and police station and when security forces converged on the town, withdrew to the local hospital. There, they took some 1,800 hostages, mostly civilians and including some 150 children.

Basayev demanded that Moscow end its operations in Chechnya and open direct negotiations with the ChRI government. He threatened to kill the hostages if the Russians moved against him, tried to prevent his access to

Shamil Basayev (in green devotional headband) among hostages in the hospital of Budyonnovsk in June 1994, during the raid that essentially brought an end to the first war. (VLADIMIR MASHATIN/AFP via Getty Images)

the media, or refused to accept his terms. Several times, government forces tried to storm the building but were driven back. Eventually Russian prime minister Viktor Chernomyrdin personally negotiated a resolution that in effect granted the Chechens their demands. On 19 June, Basayev and his remaining fighters, accompanied by over 100 volunteer hostages, including journalists and parliamentarians, were allowed back into Chechnya. Much of Budyonnovsk was in ruins, 147 people were dead (many from Russian fire), but perhaps most comprehensively shattered was Moscow's confidence and its claims that the war in Chechnya was going easily to be won. Chernomyrdin was no dove, but seizing the moment while Yeltsin was away at a conference in Canada, he was shrewd enough to know when to cut a deal.

Basayev's men had suffered just 12 casualties, yet their act of terrorism had not only humbled their enemies – FSK director Sergei Stepashin and Interior Minister Viktor Yerin, both hawks, were forced to resign because of the mismanagement of the crisis – it had changed the course of the conflict. It did not end the war, but it demonstrated convincingly that the Russians were asymmetrically vulnerable to unexpected threats. Nevertheless, although negotiations and ceasefires came and went over following months, something of a bloody stalemate seemed to be emerging. The Chechens could not dislodge the federal forces, nor, as in history, meet them in open battle. However, the Russians were unable to bring their forces properly to bear on the rebels and end the war.

The rebels could take back territory, just not hold it. On 20 August 1995, rebels under field commander Allaudin Khamzatov captured the strategic town of Argun, east of Grozny, from a mixed army and MVD garrison. They held it for just two hours, before slipping away into the nearby hills as a relief force was being desperately scrambled. They took almost no losses, and while the attack would seem to have been pointless, it heartened the rebels, embarrassed the Russian commanders, and shook their troops. A more serious example was the battle of Gudermes in December 1995. On 14 December, the very day Chechens were meant to be voting for their new – Moscow-approved – republican president, some 600 rebels under Salman Raduyev attacked the country's second largest city. They managed to take large tracts of central Gudermes, considered one of the most secure federal strongholds in Chechnya, although they were not able to storm its military headquarters. For two weeks, federal forces launched repeated assaults, interspersed with artillery barrages, but while Raduyev's men could not expand their grip on the city, nor were the Russians able to break them. Eventually, a local ceasefire was agreed and Raduyev and his forces were allowed safe passage out of the city. Gudermes returned to federal hands, but at the price of allowing the rebels out to fight another day.

That they did. On 9 January 1996, Raduyev led some 200 fighters into neighbouring Dagestan to attack the airbase at Kizlyar. They only destroyed two helicopters there – most were elsewhere or on operations – but when federal forces responded, seemingly more quickly than

he had anticipated, Raduyev took a leaf out of Basayev's playbook. His men retreated to the nearby town, took over 1,000 hostages and holed up in the city hospital and an adjacent building. A deal was struck allowing them to return to Chechnya in return for the hostages. Most were let go, with some 150 kept as human shields. However, the Russians were not willing to let Raduyev strike a third time. Just short of the border, the Chechen convoy came under fire from a helicopter and the guerrillas seized the nearby village of Pervomayskoye, taking more hostages and digging in.

There followed three days of sporadic assaults by Russian special forces, which led to heavy casualties on their side but no progress. They resorted to bombarding the village, claiming that the hostages had already been killed, while commanders competed to put the blame on others and some units seemed on the verge of mutiny. On the eighth night, though, most of the surviving Chechens managed to break through the Russian lines and flee, assisted by a diversionary attack launched by other rebel forces which had come to support them. Raduyev was among them, and would continue to elude the Russians until his capture in 2000; he died in the Russian Bely Lebed ('White Swan') maximum-security prison camp in 2002.

The Kizlyar/Pervomayskoye operation encapsulated the dynamics on both sides. The Chechens retained the initiative, and could win when they struck unexpectedly. They also still had forces with the morale, weapons and will to fight. On the other hand, their 'army' was shattering into various autonomous forces under charismatic warlords who often had their own agendas. Dudayev, after all, would contradict himself as to whether he had or had not ordered the Kizlyar attack. Raduyev, though, was one of a new generation who had little time for negotiation or moderation; whereas many of his colleagues would drift into Islamic extremism, he simply seems to have lived for the fight, whatever the costs. He had no qualms about extending the war beyond Chechnya's borders, nor over merging war

OPPOSITE
Rebel warlord Salman Raduyev in the Dagestani village of Pervomayskoye during his January 1996 cross-border raid. He is using a satellite phone in his abortive negotiations with the authorities. (AFP via Getty Images)

and terrorism. Meanwhile, the Russians were still slow to respond. They were also deeply divided over tactics and aims and also between institutions and officers. Many within the military, especially veterans of Afghanistan, believed that they should withdraw. Others felt that Yermolov's policies of ethnic cleansing were needed. Meanwhile, with no clear sense of direction and no strong political pressure encouraging them to consider Chechen hearts and mind, they too often relied on indiscriminate firepower to solve any problem. In the process, while rebels were dying, others were joining up. In part this was because actions such as Budyonnovsk, Gudermes and Kizlyar were considered victories by some, but it was also in part because often-brutal Russian tactics helped galvanize resistance. In a country where avenging fallen family members and slights to one kin is still a strong part of national culture, the Russians were virtually Dudayev's recruiting sergeants.

Dudayev himself, though, was hardly much of an asset to the rebel cause. He issued stirring pronouncements from time to time, but was neither a battlefield tactician, nor a negotiator able to use the sporadic and often half-hearted negotiations with the Russians to reach any kind of a deal. The 'peace plan' he proposed to Yeltsin, for example, demanded that he arrest the current and former commanders of the OGV, sack his prime minister and key security ministers and purge his parliament! Arguably Dudayev's greatest and last gift to the Chechen cause took place on 21 April 1996, when he put a satellite phone call through to a liberal parliamentarian in Moscow and was killed by Russian homing missiles for his pains. His death meant that formal power devolved to his vice president, Zelimkhan Yandarbiyev. However, this poet and children's author wielded relatively little real authority among members of the rebel movement, who instead looked to Aslan Maskhadov for leadership. He, in turn, knew that the Chechens were unlikely to win a war of attrition with the vastly more numerous Russians, especially as the latter were beginning to adapt to the circumstances of this war. Already, the new forces

Moscow had deployed were beginning to make their weight known on the battlefield. Instead, like all great guerrilla commanders, Maskhadov knew that his struggle was essentially political. Budyonnovsk had brought the Russians to negotiations, even if ultimately that chance had been squandered. He needed an equivalent, or even greater, 'spectacular' to convince Moscow to come to terms, and not an act of terror but something to demonstrate that the Chechens could also win on the battlefield. His gaze turned to Grozny.

Left to right: Chechen rebel leader Zelimkhan Yandarbiyev, spokesman Movladi Udugov and commander Shamil Basayev at a press conference near Vedeno in June 1996. (VLADIMIR MASHATIN/AFP via Getty Images)

The second battle for Grozny

On 1 January 1996, Lieutenant-General Vyacheslav Tikhomirov had been appointed head of the OGV. Tikhomirov was a career Armed Forces officer, unlike his two predecessors, Kulikov (who became interior minister after Yerin) and Lieutenant-General Shkirko (another

In February 1996, Chechen women and men pass by the destroyed presidential palace in Grozny. (Photo by ALEXANDER NEMENOV/AFP via Getty Images)

MVD VV veteran). With his arrival, the Russian forces stepped up their efforts to win on the battlefield, but in the main all that happened was that offensives would take ground, only to lose it once the tempo slackened. With Dudayev's death in April, Maskhadov was eager to seize the military and thus political initiative. Yandarbiyev's representatives and Moscow's continued arm's length, on-again, off-again talks about talks, which led to sporadic ceasefires but no real prospect of true agreement. Indeed, Yandarbiyev could not even claim to be speaking for the whole rebel movement, as Basayev said he should be deposed for talking to the Russians.

At the same time Maskhadov, who was taking an active role in peace talks being held in Nazran in Ingushetia, was also working on a fall-back option, assembling a coalition of warlords willing to take part in a daring strike. Meanwhile, the tempo of guerrilla attacks slackened somewhat, allowing the Russians to begin to think they were winning. This also allowed Moscow to make a point of doing something it had been promising to do: bring forces home. A conscript army is inevitably subject to regular rotations of units and men, and as units were withdrawn from Chechnya, they were not matched by new elements being deployed. At the end of May, Yeltsin visited Grozny – under very tight security – and told assembled soldiers from the 205th Motor Rifle Brigade, 'The war is over, you have won.' Reflecting this upbeat mood, by then federal forces had been allowed to shrink from their peak of 55,000 personnel to just over 41,000: 19,000 Armed Forces and 22,000 MVD VV, OMON and other security elements. Further reductions, especially to the Armed Forces contingent, were to follow: the aim was that eventually no more than one MVD VV brigade and the 205th Motor Rifle Brigade were to be left by the end of the year.

By July, the Russians had decided to escalate their operations in the south, hoping to force the rebels into accepting their terms. As they focused their forces to seize such remaining rebel strongholds as the village of Alkhan-Yurt, they pulled forces out of Grozny, including not just

MVD VV garrisons but also police officers of the pro-
Moscow regime. Anticipating this, though, Maskhadov
had assembled forces for what the Russians would
later claimed was called 'Operation *Jihad*' (there is no
independent confirmation of this, though, and it seems
more likely to be a clumsy attempt to paint Maskhadov
as an Islamic extremist), a daring counter-strike on
Grozny itself, timed to overshadow the inauguration of
Boris Yeltsin, who had just been re-elected to the Russian
presidency in a poll widely regarded as rigged.

On the morning of 6 August – the very day federal
forces were launching their assault on Alkhan-Yurt –
some 1,500 rebels from a number of units were quietly
infiltrating Grozny in 25-man teams. Although the
defenders had established a network of checkpoints
and guard stations, their reluctance to venture out at
night, as well as their reduced numbers, meant that
it was relatively easy for the rebels to move into their
city. At 5.50am, they struck, attacking a wide range

A Russian tank rolls
through the ruined
streets of Grozny
in August 1996.
The white cloth on
the barrel does not
denote surrender
but is a recognition
symbol, even though
by this time the
Chechens had
very little surviving
armour. (Photo
by Eric BOUVET/
Gamma-Rapho via
Getty Images)

Aslan Maskhadov

Undoubtedly the outstanding figure of the war on either side, Maskhadov was a brilliant guerrilla commander who ultimately proved unable to master the more shadowy ways of Chechen politics. Like Dudayev, he was a product of the forced dispersal of the Chechens and was born in Kazakhstan in 1951. His family returned home in 1957 and he joined the Soviet Armed Forces, serving as an artillery officer and receiving two Orders for Service to the Homeland. He retired in 1992 with the rank of colonel after a 25-year military career. Returning home, he became head of civil defence within the ChRI and then chief of staff of the ChRI military. When the Russians invaded, he co-ordinated the bitter defence of Grozny and then the subsequent – and brilliant – operation to retake the city in 1996. Following that, he assumed a new role as negotiator and peacemaker, reaching the Khasav-Yurt Accord with fellow veteran Russian Security Council chairman Alexander Lebed, paving the way for an end to the First Chechen War. He then became ChRI prime minister before winning the presidency in the elections of January 1997.

Shamil Basayev (left) conferring with Aslan Maskhadov (right) at Novogroznenskaya. The silenced AS Val Basayev carries is as much as anything else a high-prestige trophy. (SERGEY SHAKHIJANIAN/AFP via Getty Images)

He proved unequal to the challenge of administering Chechnya in a time of peace, though, faced with covert pressure from Moscow, overt challenges from jihadists and the practical problems of rebuilding a country in ruins without revenue. Unable to defeat the Islamic extremists, he tried to conciliate them with a formal introduction of *sharia* law in 1999, but ultimately he was always a secular nationalist at heart and this was too little, too late. He was caught between an increasingly hard-line Moscow, with the rise of then Prime Minister Putin, and increasingly hard-line jihadists. When Shamil Basayev and Emir Khattab unilaterally invaded Dagestan in 1999, giving Putin the excuse he needed, Maskhadov's efforts to avert war were doomed.

During the Second Chechen War, Maskhadov did his duty, but his authority over Chechen forces was increasingly weak thanks to the efforts of the jihadists. He tried several times to reopen peace talks, but to no avail. He was equally unsuccessful in seeking to prevent the use of terrorism by Basayev and his allies. In 2005, he died during a commando attack by FSB forces on a hideout in the town of Tolstoy-Yurt. Although accounts are unclear, it is likely he died at the hand of his nephew and bodyguard, Viskhan Hadzhimuradov, who had orders to shoot him rather than let him be captured.

of strategic targets including the municipal building, Khankala airbase, Grozny airport and the headquarters of the police and the FSB, as well as closing key transport arteries. They placed mines in some garrisons and set up firing stations to command the routes along which federal forces could sally.

Within three hours, most of the city was in Chechen hands, or at least out of meaningful federal control. Although Russian forces and their Chechen allies (who had a particular fear of being captured) were holding out in the centre, around the republican MVD and FSB buildings and also at Khankala, the speed and daring of the attack led to disarray and downright panic among the numerically superior defenders. There had been some 7,000 Armed Forces and MVD VV personnel in Grozny, but most fled or simply hunkered down in their garrisons. The rebels did execute some collaborators and also in several cases refused to take prisoners, especially of pro-Moscow Chechen forces. However, in the main

Two women pull whatever they can salvage from a shattered Grozny, joining the tens of thousands of refugees displaced by the siege. (ALEXANDER NEMENOV/AFP via Getty Images)

they were happy to let people flee: they wanted the city and knew large numbers of captives would only tie down their own, outnumbered forces. Nevertheless, perhaps 5,000 federal troops would remain penned within the city, unable or unwilling to try to break out.

Besides, the rebels' numbers only grew as news of this daring attack spread. Some pro-Moscow Chechens switched sides, some city residents took up arms and further reinforcements arrived from across Chechnya. Desperate to regain the city, the Russians did not wait to gather their forces but instead threw them into the city piecemeal as soon as they became available, allowing Maskhadov to defeat them in detail. On 7 August, a reinforced battalion from the 205th Motor Rifle Brigade was beaten back and another armoured column was ambushed and shattered the next day. On 11 August, a battalion from the 276th Motor Rifle

Regiment managed to make it through to the defenders at the centre of the city, delivering some supplies and evacuating a few of the wounded, but they failed to make a real breakthrough.

After another week of desultory clashes, the city remained largely in rebel hands. Their numbers had grown to some 6,000 fighters, while around 3,000–4,000 federals were still trapped behind their lines. Lieutenant-General Konstantin Pulikovsky, acting commander of the OGV while Tikhomirov was on a singularly ill-timed holiday, lost his patience and on 19 August issued an ultimatum demanding that the rebels surrender Grozny within 48 hours or an all-out assault would be launched. Even before that ultimatum had expired, next day air and artillery bombardments began and the flow of refugees out of the city increased dramatically. By 21 August, an estimated 220,000 people had fled Grozny, leaving no more than 70,000 civilians in a city which before the war had been home to 400,000.

The pugnacious General Alexander Lebed (right), surrounded by his bodyguards, in talks with Shirvany Basayev, brother of Shamil, on 31 August 1996, as a preliminary to formal peace talks. (Photo by ALEXANDER NEMENOV/AFP via Getty Images)

A moment of
reflection as Russian
soldiers remember
their dead comrades
in November 1999.
(REUTERS)

However, the ability of the Chechen rebels, long described as a defeated and dwindling force, to retake Grozny had a dramatic impact on Russian politics. Even while Pulikovsky was gathering forces for a massive bombardment of Grozny that would have led to casualties among federal forces, civilians and rebels alike, opinion against the war in Moscow was hardening. Although a number of politicians had long expressed their doubts, the crucial constituency was that of disgruntled Armed Forces officers, especially veterans of Afghanistan, who

saw Chechnya as an equally unwinnable and pointless
war. Such figures as General Boris Gromov (former last
commander of the 40th Army in Afghanistan) had long
been calling for a withdrawal. However, the prospect of
massive friendly fire and civilian casualties in Grozny
galvanized the highest-profile member of this camp,
Security Council secretary (and Soviet–Afghan War
veteran) Alexander Lebed. A blunt, even tactless man
nevertheless idolized by the VDV troops who served
with him, Lebed had been decorated for his service in

Afghanistan and had refused to back communist hard-liners during the 1991 August Coup when they ordered him to deploy his 106th Airborne Division against Yeltsin's supporters. In the June presidential elections he had come third with 14.5 per cent of the vote, but then threw his weight behind Yeltsin in the run-off poll, in return being appointed to the politically pivotal role of secretary of the Security Council and Yeltsin's national security adviser. If Yeltsin had thought this would tame the outspoken Lebed, he was wrong, but by the same token Yeltsin was clearly in poor physical health and was worried that the Communist Party might be able to make a renewed bid for power. He was eager, too, to extricate himself from a war that seemed now to have no end.

On 20 August, Lebed returned to Chechnya and ordered federal forces around Chechnya and in the south alike to stand down and observe a ceasefire. Thanks to the assistance of the OSCE, he opened direct talks with Maskhadov and on 30 August they concluded the Khasav-Yurt Accord. This shelved the question of Chechnya's constitutional status but instead recognized Chechen autonomy and a full withdrawal of all federal forces by 31 December. Further treaties would follow, which would formalize Maskhadov's willingness to cede claims of outright independence for an end to the fighting and an unprecedented level of autonomy within the Russian Federation. In effect, so long as Chechnya pretended to be part of Russia, Moscow would not try to assert any actual control over it. The First Chechen War was over.

The price was high, though. According to official figures, Russia had lost 3,860 soldiers and another 1,872 MVD personnel, for a total of 5,732, with another 17,862 wounded. However, the independent Committee of Soldiers' Mothers put the figure of dead and missing at more than 14,000. Even military sources later tacitly accept that the real tally was closer to theirs, probably because the government numbers only count those confirmed as dead, not simply missing. Even Kulikov, no dove, acknowledged that the figures were being massaged:

Let me tell you about one specific case. I knew for sure that on this day – it was at the end of February or the beginning of March 1995 – 40 servicemen… were killed. And they brought me information about 15. I asked: 'Why don't you take into account the rest?' They hesitated: 'Well, you see, 40 is a lot. We'd better spread those losses over a few days.'

Conversely, while the Kremlin claimed more than 17,000 rebels had been killed, most independent analyses put the real number closer to the Chechens' own figure of 3,000. Arguably a more serious price to be paid was political, as the Kremlin faced humiliation for its defeat, while the Chechen leadership would struggle to turn a wartime coalition into a working new government.

The 'hot peace', 1996–99

For the Grozny operation, Maskhadov had had to assemble a coalition of warlords, commanding some, haggling and negotiating with the rest, including Akhmad Zakayev, Doku Umarov and Ruslan Gelayev. This was a warning sign, that Chechen politics had already become fractured between rival leaders, clans, factions and platforms. Maskhadov would discover that navigating Chechen politics would prove every bit as difficult, as well as dangerous, as fighting the war. In October, President Yandarbiyev formally appointed him prime minister of the ChRI and in January 1997 Maskhadov was elected president in a landslide victory, winning over 59 per cent of the vote. Radical warlord Shamil Basayev came second with 23.5 per cent, Yandarbiyev received only 10 per cent and none of the other 17 candidates could top even 1 per cent. Translating this vote of confidence into real power, though, was the challenge.

In May 1997, Maskhadov travelled to Moscow, signing the final peace accord with Yeltsin. But peace did not mean amity, and not only would there be those in both Russia and Chechnya who wanted to resume

Left to right: Movlady Udugov, Russian Security Council secretary Ivan Rybkin and Akhmed Zakayev look on as Boris Yeltsin and Aslan Maskhadov sign the peace treaty in Moscow on 12 May 1997. (STR/AFP via Getty Images)

hostilities; the challenge of rebuilding this shattered country was formidable. Moscow was not willing to pay reparations and the cost of reconstruction was estimated at $300 million. Unemployment reached 80 per cent and pensions and similar benefits simply were not being paid.

Maskhadov did what he could, but that often was not very much. He could not disarm the warlords, so instead he brought them into the ChRI's military structure, granting them ranks and official status in the hope that it would tame them. In the main, it did not. Some became virtual local dictators and bandit chieftains, such as Arbi Barayev. A police officer who then became Yandarbiyev's bodyguard, Barayev set up his own unit during the war, calling it the Special Purpose Islamic Regiment. Even then, though, he became notorious for his bloodthirstiness and his kidnap operations. After the war, although he and his 'regiment' were formally inducted into the ChRI Interior Ministry, he set himself up near Urus-Martan and turned to protection racketeering and kidnap for ransom. Barayev refused to subordinate himself to the interior minister or stop his extracurricular activities and in 1998 there was even an armed clash between his men and Chechen security forces in Gudermes. Barayev was stripped of his rank of brigadier-general but continued to have the loyalty of his men and so maintained his personal fiefdom in south-central Chechnya. He arranged for the murder of the head of the police's anti-kidnap unit and even made two attempts to have Maskhadov assassinated.

Barayev was perhaps the worst of several such local warlords, but his case also illustrates the second key challenge to Maskhadov: the rise of jihadist extremists. After all, while Barayev was not an especially pious man, one reason why he was able to survive as long as he did is that he was able to find common cause with the jihadists against the moderate nationalist Maskhadov. Indeed, Maskhadov blamed Barayev for the kidnap of four Western telecommunications engineers in 1998 (three Britons and a New Zealander) and the likelihood is that they were killed because Osama bin Laden outbid the engineers' company and wanted them decapitated as a political gesture, instead.

After all, the influence of the jihadists had increased during the 1990s. In the early 1990s, when travel was easier, a number of ethnic Chechens from Jordan, descendants of earlier refugees and forced migrants, visited the country. One was Fathi Mohammed Habib, an ageing veteran of the Soviet–Afghan War. He settled in Chechnya in 1993 and became the first link connecting wider Salafist extremist Islamic communities with local radicals (whom the Russians call Wahhabis). His most divisive legacy was to invite the Saudi-born al-Qaeda field commander Emir Khattab to Chechnya. Born Thamir Saleh Abdullah Al-Suwailem, Khattab had fought against the Soviets in Afghanistan, where he met Osama bin Laden and became an al-Qaeda troubleshooter, seeing action in Tajikistan, Azerbaijan and the former Yugoslavia. In 1995, he entered Chechnya under the guise of a journalist and began training Chechens as well as distributing funds and weapons provided by al-Qaeda. He was an effective guerrilla commander, but his real strength was as a politician. Thanks to his combination of charisma, experience and resources, he became increasingly close to several key rebel figures, most notably Zelimkhan Yandarbiyev (who awarded him the Chechen Order of the Brave Warrior) and Shamil Basayev. Khattab mistrusted Maskhadov – a sentiment that was heartily returned – and was probably behind several of the assassination attempts against him.

Russian Army D-30 howitzers pound Shamil Basayev's forces during their ill-fated incursion into Dagestan. (Photo by Antoine GYORI/Sygma via Getty Images)

However, Khattab was protected by both Basayev and Yandarbiyev, was paying off many of the more mercenary warlords and had his own force of predominantly Arab fighters. Maskhadov could not afford to turn on him.

Khattab made no effort to conceal his true goal, which was not Chechen independence, but to raise a general *jihad* across the North Caucasus to drive out Christian Russia and create an Islamic caliphate. To this

end, he denounced the Khasav-Yurt Accord and actively tried to undermine it. In December 1997, he and his forces even took part, alongside Dagestani insurgents, in a cross-border raid against the 136th Armoured Brigade headquarters in Buynaksk. Maskhadov was forced to deny any Chechens were involved but still he could not afford to trigger a civil war by moving directly against him. The next year Khattab and Basayev formally joined forces, establishing the 'International Islamic Peacekeeping Brigade'.

Maskhadov tried to hold the country together, but with diminishing success. The economy was still disastrous and people were disillusioned with peace. In July 1998, after the fourth assassination attempt on Maskhadov, he declared a state of emergency, but his capacities to crack down on the estimated 300 separate armed groups numbering a total of around 8,500 men in the country was limited, not least because any that he targeted could turn to the jihadists for support. He then tried to reconcile the increasingly powerful jihadists by going against his own secular tendencies and introducing *sharia* law, but they were not willing to compromise. Instead, this simply led to splits within the Chechen government and an increasing sense of disillusionment among Maskhadov's core supporters.

All that was needed was a spark, and Khattab and Basayev were determined to provide one. Neighbouring Dagestan had been experiencing its own rise in anti-Russian and jihadist violence. In April, Bagauddin Magomedov, self-proclaimed 'Emir of the Islamic Jamaat [Movement] of Dagestan', and an ally of Khattab's, had appealed for a *gazavat* to 'free Dagestan'. On 7 August 1999, Khattab and Basayev led a mixed force of some 1,500 Chechen, Dagestani and Arab fighters across the border, proclaimed the 'Islamic State of Dagestan' and began advancing on Botlikh, the nearest town.

Federal forces were characteristically slow in responding, but – just like those federal forces when they invaded Chechnya – the International Islamic Peacekeeping Brigade would face a rude awakening.

Magomedov had assured them they would be welcomed as liberators, but instead they were met not only by tenacious Dagestani police, but also spontaneous resistance from ordinary locals. This helped slow the invaders down long enough for the inevitable deluge of Russian firepower. The attack stalled and, in the face of combined ground and air attacks, was forced back into Chechnya. A mix of Armed Forces units, the MVD VV's 102nd Brigade, Dagestani OMON and Russian *Spetsnaz* demonstrated a level of competence that had rarely been seen in the First Chechen War. On 5 September, a second incursion was launched further north, striking towards Khasav-Yurt, but this too was blocked after an initial surprise advance, then driven back by local and federal forces. The Russians launched cross-border bombing raids first to try to strike the rebels as they withdrew and then to punish the Maskhadov government for letting this happen, as the attacks shifted to Grozny.

Maskhadov had realized the danger of the attacks and condemned them from the first. He announced a crackdown on Khattab and Basayev and pledged to restore discipline over the warlords. It was too little, too late. After all, there were also rising forces in Moscow looking to reassert control over Chechnya. Khattab and Basayev wanted a war: Vladimir Putin would give them one.

Putin's war: the invasion

Russia in 1999 was a rather different country from 1994 or even 1996. Yeltsin's failing health and political grip had led him to search for a successor who could secure his legacy (and look after him and his circle, known as 'the family'). The chosen figure was a relatively little-known administrator and former spy from St Petersburg called Vladimir Putin. A career officer in the Soviet KGB, in 1990 Putin returned to Russia from East Germany and from 1991 began working within the local administration. He acquired a reputation as a tough, discreet and efficient fixer, working for the mayor before being called to Moscow to work at first in the presidential

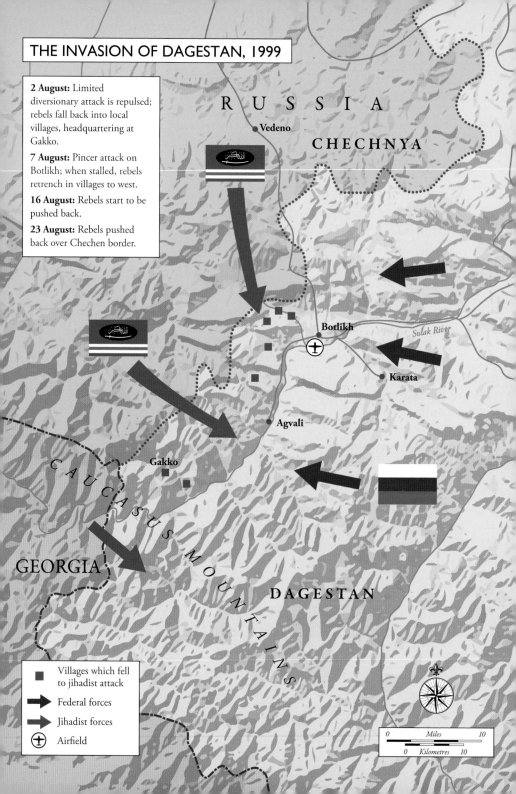

THE INVASION OF DAGESTAN, 1999

2 August: Limited diversionary attack is repulsed; rebels fall back into local villages, headquartering at Gakko.

7 August: Pincer attack on Botlikh; when stalled, rebels retrench in villages to west.

16 August: Rebels start to be pushed back.

23 August: Rebels pushed back over Chechen border.

RUSSIA

CHECHNYA

Vedeno

Botlikh

Sulak River

Karata

Agvali

Gakko

CAUCASUS MOUNTAINS

GEORGIA

DAGESTAN

■ Villages which fell to jihadist attack

➤ Federal forces

➤ Jihadist forces

✛ Airfield

0 ___ Miles ___ 10

0 ___ Kilometres ___ 10

administration; he became head of the FSB in 1998 and then acting prime minister on 9 August 1999. Yeltsin announced that he wanted Putin to be his successor; on 31 December, he unexpectedly stepped down, making Putin acting president, further strengthening his hand for the March 2000 presidential elections, which Putin won with a comfortable 53 per cent of the vote.

A nationalist and a statist, Putin made no secret of his desire to reverse the weakening of central control under Yeltsin and his determination to make the world recognize Russia as a great power once again. He had also enjoyed a meteoric rise thanks to powerful patrons within the system but was relatively unknown to the Russian public; he needed some high-profile triumph, some dramatic opportunity to prove that the Kremlin was now occupied by a determined and powerful leader. Chechnya seemed perfect for this. While Khattab and Basayev were giving him the grounds to tear up the treaty with Grozny with their incursion into Dagestan, he began instructing his generals to prepare for a second war. Contingency plans for an invasion had, after all, started to be developed in March and for over a year the Russian military had been actively wargaming invasion plans. In July 1998, for example, an exercise across the North Caucasus saw 15,000 Armed Forces and MVD troops practise fighting against 'terrorists'.

Putin was determined that this time the Russians would muster adequate forces, prepare properly and plan for a guerrilla war. Furthermore, the Russian public would be readied for the inevitable casualties. In September, a mysterious series of bombs exploded in apartment buildings in Moscow (twice), Buynaksk and Volgodonsk, killing 293 people. Still to this day there is controversy over these bombs. There is certainly a serious body of belief that these were provocations arranged by the Russian security agencies, not least given that a similar bomb was found by chance in Ryazan and connected to the FSB, which then claimed this had been a training drill. Nevertheless, the Kremlin presented this as an escalation of the Chechens' terror campaign and at the time many ordinary Russians were frightened and angry, looking to the government for security and revenge.

The bombing campaign which had followed the Dagestani incursion was expanded steadily, hammering Chechen cities until the flood of refugees into Ingushetia was exceeding 5,000 people a day. Overall, perhaps a quarter of the total remaining Chechen population would flee and while this put great pressure on neighbouring regions to deal with the influx of refugees, drawing on Mao's famous analogy that guerrillas move among the population like fish in the sea, it also drained much of the 'sea' to allow the Russians to spot the 'fish' that much more easily. 'Filtration camps' were established behind the army lines, to hold and process refugees, identifying suspected rebels for interrogation and detention (not least, by checking for the distinctive bruises on right knee and shoulder that would suggest the use of an assault rifle or rocket launcher).

On 1 October, Putin formally declared Maskhadov and the Chechen government illegitimate and reasserted the authority of the Russian Federation over its wayward subject. Meanwhile, federal forces started moving. Instead of the foolhardy direct assault of the first war, the Russian plan was a staged and methodical one. The first stage was as far as possible to seal Chechnya's borders, while forces were assembled. All told, these numbered some 50,000 Armed Forces troops and a further 40,000 MVD VV and OMON personnel, some three times as many men as had taken part in the 1994 invasion. Overall command went to Colonel-General Viktor Kazantsev, commander of the North Caucasus Military District.

Then, Moscow announced that in the interests of securing the border and establishing a 'cordon sanitaire', units would have to take up positions which 'in a few cases' would be 'up to five kilometres' (3 miles) inside northern Chechnya. Then, saying that the terrain meant that it was impossible to secure this line, they warned that they would advance as far as the Terek River, occupying the northern third of the country. By 5 October, they had taken these new positions. Fighting was at this stage sporadic and localized, in part because Maskhadov was still trying to make peace. Again, the Russians were in no rush. They spent the next week consolidating their forces – and ignoring Maskhadov's overtures – until 12 October, when they crossed the Terek, pushing towards Grozny in three fronts. The Western Group pushed through the Nadterechnaya district until it reached the western suburbs of Grozny; the Northern Group pushed down across the Terek at Chervlennaya; while the Eastern Group swung past Gudermes and likewise moved to flank Grozny from the east. As they advanced, the federal forces met relatively little resistance, with local settlements' community leaders often protesting their loyalty and claiming that there were no rebels in their areas. These settlements would be searched for weapons and fugitives and then MVD forces would establish guard posts. Where the Russians did come under fire, they would typically fall back and liberally use artillery and air power to clear potential threats and obstacles in their path before continuing.

The Second Chechen War was in many ways the making of Vladimir Putin, shown here while still prime minister in December 1999. (AFP via Getty Images)

On 15 October, they seized the Tersky Heights, which commanded Grozny from the north-west. Accepting that no truce was possible, Maskhadov declared martial law and called for a *gazavat* against the Russians. Within the next few days, the Russians slowly encircled the city, taking outlying towns and villages such as Goragorsky (one of Shamil Basayev's bases) and Dolinsky. Meanwhile, Grozny itself came under sporadic but heavy bombardment, including strikes by OTR-21 Tochka short-range ballistic missiles with conventional warheads, one of which hit a marketplace on 21 October, killing more than 140 civilians.

Again in contrast to the first war, the Russians were willing to leave Grozny until they had consolidated their rear. In this, they were also the beneficiaries of the years of in-fighting within Chechnya, which had broken the discipline that had held the rebels together before. Gudermes, for example, fell to the Russians to a large extent because of the defection of the Yamadayevs, the dominant local family of the Benoi *teip*, who had their own private army (known officially as the 2nd ChRI National Guard Battalion). Pragmatists, the Yamadayevs had been very much on the secular, nationalist wing of the rebels. In 1998, they had clashed with Arbi Barayev and units of the jihadist Sharia Regiment and might have destroyed them, had pressure not been brought to bear to arrange a ceasefire. Squeezed between an increasingly jihadist rebel movement and the approaching federal forces, the Yamadayevs opted to make a deal with the Russians. Their forces would become the basis of the Vostok (East) Battalion, set up by the GRU (Military Intelligence) and commanded first by Dzhabrail

A Russian 2S9 Nona 120mm self-propelled gun-mortar system pounding Grozny in November 1999 during the siege of the city. (REUTERS)

Yamadayev and then his brother Sulim. They would not be the only defectors.

Through November and December, the Russians concentrated on taking and holding urban centres, forcing the rebels either to cede them and be forced into the countryside during the bitter North Caucasus winter, or else to stand and fight where they could be battered by federal firepower. The village of Bamut, which had held out for 18 months in the first war, fell on 17 November, bombed and shelled to rubble. Argun fell on 2 December, Urus-Martan on 8 December. In December, the federal forces turned to Shali, the last rebel-held town outside Grozny, which had fallen by the end of the year, although efforts were made by the rebels to retake it and Argun in January.

The third battle of Grozny

The defenders had had time to fortify Grozny. They dug trenches, laid mines, built fortified positions inside some buildings and booby-trapped others. However, the Russians were also far more prepared for the latest battle of Grozny. Chief of the General Staff General Anatoly Kvashnin, who had been responsible for the initial and disastrous New Year's Eve attack on Grozny in 1994, was determined to atone for his earlier failure. Beyond a few skirmishes and probing raids, though October, November and much of December, the Russians confined themselves to bombardments using aircraft, Scud and OTR-21 ballistic missiles, artillery and TOS-1 fuel air explosive rockets. Only some 40,000 civilians were left in the ruins of the city, along with perhaps 2,500 rebels under Aslambek Ismailov. On 5 December, the Russians starting dropping leaflets, urging those remaining to leave by 11 December, while opening up a safe corridor for them. Although many Chechens mistrusted this offer, not least as the Russians checked the documents of those leaving, there was no mistaking that the Russians were preparing for an assault.

They mustered some 5,000 troops for the assault itself: the 506th Motor Rifle Regiment, two MVD

VV brigades and in total some 400–500 *Spetsnaz*, who were particularly used for reconnaissance, sniper and counter-sniper duties. They were backed by extensive artillery elements and OMON (who would be used for rear-area security). In what was a portent of the future, they were also supported by some 2,000 pro-Moscow (or at least anti-rebel) Chechen fighters in a militia commanded by Beslan Gantemirov, a convicted embezzler whom Yeltsin had pardoned in return for his becoming the mayor of Grozny in the new regime. He recruited a force of volunteers, patriots, mercenaries, opportunists and criminals whom the federals trusted little – the MVD only issued them out-dated AKM-47s from reserve stocks, which had been phased out of military use in the 1980s – but who nevertheless knew the city and were fierce and flexible, like their ChRI counterparts.

The siege forces started moving in on 12 December, infiltrating reconnaissance elements to draw rebel fire and then hammering the rebels with airstrikes and artillery. By the end of the next day, Khankala airbase was back in federal hands. One exploratory push into Minutka Square by the 506th was ambushed, although the new T-90 tank proved much more resistant to RPGs than the old T-80 had, one surviving seven hits. The fighting was fierce: about a quarter of the soldiers of the 506th were killed or wounded, so it was withdrawn and replaced with fresh troops of the 423rd Guards 'Yampolsky' Motor Rifle Regiment. In the main, though, the Russians were content to draw their ring slowly closer. That put the pressure on the Chechens to seek to break out or distract the federal forces with other attacks. This they did, in one case managing to take back the outlying village of Alkhan-Kala, but each time they did so, they took casualties they could not afford and, thanks to the siege of the city, could not replace.

On 15 January, Kazantsev decided the ground had been prepared well enough. Federal forces moved into the city along three axes, facing both tough rebel resistance from the 2,500 or so remaining defenders as well as the problems in trying to move through a city not only liberally strewn with mines, traps and unexploded ordnance but also pounded into rubble. This, along with the Russians' new-found caution, kept advances slow. Even so, the rebels were able frequently to infiltrate the Russian lines, lay more mines and stage lightning attacks, in one case managing to kill Major-General Mikhail Malofeyev, commander of the Northern Group, in the assault. Nevertheless, the best they could do was slow the Russian advance. By the end of the month, running low on men, ground to retreat into and ammunition, the rebel commanders opted to abandon the city, regroup at the village of Alkhan-Kala south-west of Grozny and make for the highlands in the hope of regrouping and

Mortars were indispensable sources of short-range firepower. Here, a Russian soldier in winter kit loads a shell during the battle for Duba-Yurt, south of Grozny, in January 2000. (UPI / Alamy Stock Photo)

The BMP-2 was a considerable improvement on its predecessor, but even so Russian troops often preferred to ride on top, to avoid being trapped inside if their carrier hit a mine. (UPI / Alamy Stock Photo)

following the same trajectory as in the First Chechen War. Already, though, the new divisiveness of the rebel movement was becoming visible, as Ruslan Gelayev – following a disagreement with the jihadist elements of the rebel command – withdrew his forces from the city, allowing them to slip out in small groups all around the perimeter.

At the end of January, as federal forces continued to grind into the centre of Grozny, the rebels attempted to break out of the city under the cover of a heavy storm.

Some tried to bribe their way through Russian lines, others to slip out hidden among groups of refugees, while others tried to use stealth when possible, firepower when not. This would be a disastrous and humiliating flight, as rebels blundered into minefields outside Alkhan-Kala, were scoured by artillery-fired cluster rounds (in some cases bringing Russian fire down onto civilians, too) and were harried by helicopters and Spetsnaz. Of the perhaps 1,500 rebel fighters left in Grozny, some 600 were killed, captured or wounded in the retreat, including Ismailov.

The survivors largely scattered, some simply drifting home, most heading south.

Meanwhile, on 6 February the Russians formally declared Grozny 'liberated'. Even so, the city was in ruins and it would take a month for OMON and Gantemirov's militia to mop up a few remaining hold-outs in the city and fully a year for all the bodies from the battle to be found and buried. Although on 21 February the traditional Defender of the Fatherland Day parade

was held in central Grozny, supposedly as a mark of the return of normalcy, this would be a brutal, vengeful time, as apartments were looted, men accused of being rebels were dragged off to a filtration camp (or simply shot in the street) and stray rebels continued to mount bomb and sniper attacks. The 21,000 civilians remaining of the city's Soviet-era population of 400,000 were often forced to camp out in the ruins, eating whatever they could scavenge.

Grozny in April 2000, after the indiscriminate Russian bombardment and assault that left most of the city in ruins. (Str/EPA/ Shutterstock)

Putin's war: the pacification

Grozny was the last major urban centre to fall and the federal forces quickly moved towards consolidating their positions across the country. Even while Grozny was under siege, the Russians had been pushing forwards on two separate fronts. The first was in the south, where Armed Forces units were trying to break into the southern highland strongholds. The second front was in the rear, where the MVD was establishing its own network of strong-points and garrisons of VV and OMON personnel, as well as launching aggressive patrols and search operations to locate rebels, arms caches and safe houses. With the shattering of resistance in Grozny, these other federal forces were well placed to block, intercept, capture or eliminate larger concentrations of rebels.

In April 2000, Colonel-General Gennady Troshev was appointed head of the OGV. Although the Russians were still estimating that there were some 2,000–2,500 rebels, they were satisfied that they were largely scattered around the country and posed relatively little serious challenge to federal control. They were both wrong and right. Wrong in that rebels still could cohere in units numbering several hundred and engage in operations which could cause serious Russian casualties. Right, though, in that these attacks never posed a serious threat to the federal forces' overall grip on the country. For example, one of the last major, pitched engagements of the war took place in March, at Komsomolskoye, a village south of Grozny and the home village of warlord Ruslan Gelayev. An OMON unit from Russia's Yaroslavl Region first encountered Gelayev and his men there, as they prepared to break through to the cover of the Argun Gorge. Once their numbers became clear – estimates ranged from 500 to 1,000, but the real figure was closer to the lower end of that scale – the OMON settled for trapping them in the city and calling for support. The OMON unit was promptly reinforced by an MVD VV regiment and OMON and special police units from Irkutsk, Kursk and Voronezh. After four days of almost constant bombardment, including sorties by Su-25 ground-attack jets and salvoes from TOS-1 220mm multiple rocket launchers firing thermobaric rounds, the federal forces stormed the village. The fighting was fierce and unpredictable, even though a wounded Gelayev managed to slip out of the village, and it took another week and a further bombardment before Komsomolskoye was pacified. This was one of the bloodiest battles of the war, with the official butcher's bill being 552 Chechens and more than 50 Russians. The village itself was all but levelled; journalist Anna Politkovskaya called it 'a monstrous conglomerate of burnt houses, ruins, and new graves at the cemetery', though she put the blame not just on federal forces but also Gelayev, wondering 'how could he ever think of taking the war home, to Komsomolskoye, knowing in advance that his own home village would be destroyed?'

This was a serious clash, but hardly something to make Putin think twice. Ambushes continued, sometimes substantial ones in which the Chechens could muster as many as 100 fighters and could inflict distinct losses. Even Russian airpower, which was used much more widely and effectively than in the first war,

Russian troops attack rebel positions on the outskirts of the village of Komsomolskoye, last stronghold of the warlord Ruslan Gelayev, in March 2000. (Stringer/EPA/Shutterstock)

INVASION AND CONQUEST, 1999–2006

W Western Group
N Northern Group
E Eastern Group

☐ Occupied by 5 October 1999
☐ Occupied by 31 October 1999
☐ Occupied by 31 December 1999
☐ Assault on Grozny: 15 January–
   6 February 2000
☐ Highland territory left for
   subsequent pacification

RUSSIA

STAVROPOL

Achikulak

Kochubey

Mozdok

Kamyshev

CHECHNYA

Staryy River

Pervomayskoye
Kizlyar

Dubovskaya
Kargalinskaya

Novyy
Terek
River

Naurskaya

Kalinovskaya

Nadterechnaya
Goragorsky

Terek River

Chervlennaya

Malgobek

INGUSHETIA

Sunzha River

Satsita

Dolinsky

N 4
Tolstoy-Yurt

W

GROZNY
Alkhan-Kala

Gudermes

Kadi-Yurt

Khasav-Yurt

Beslan

Nazran

Assinovskaya

Alkhan-Yurt

1

Argun

5

E

MAGAS
Ali-Yurt

B

Bamut

Urus-Martan

Khankala airbase

Shali

6

Gekhi-Chu

Komsomolskoye

A

Novye Atagi

Nozhay-Yurt

2
Zandak

Vladikavkaz

Khatuni

Vedeno

Argun River

Kirovauya

Shatoy
Sovetskoye

DAGESTAN

Sulak River

CAUCASUS MOUNTAINS

Botlikh

0   Miles   25
0   Kilometres   25

Major actions
Ⓐ Komsomolskoye, 6–24 March 2000
Ⓑ Nazran raid, 21–22 June 2004

Deaths of rebel leaders
① Arbi Barayev, 22 June 2001
② Emir Khattab, 20 March 2002
③ Ruslan Gelayev, 28 February 2004
④ Aslan Maskhadov, 8 March 2005
⑤ Abdul-Halim Sadulayev, 17 June 2006
⑥ Shamil Basayev, 10 July 2006

③

Federal garrisons
The federal forces maintained garrisons in Grozny (two
MVD VV brigades and one Army brigade), Gudermes (the
Vostok Battalion plus an MVD VV regiment), Urus-Martan
(an MDV VV regiment), Vedeno (an MVD VV battalion),
Kargalinskaya (the Zapad Battalion) and also Argun,
Nadterechnaya and Shali (one Army battalion each).

was not always decisive or invulnerable. The crash of a Su-24MR reconnaissance aircraft near the village of Benoi-Vedeno in May 2000, for example, was officially ascribed to pilot error in dense fog, but persistent reports suggest that it was hit by one of the rebels' rare Igla (SA-24) anti-air missiles. Another would be used to inflict a terrible blow in August 2002, when one of the gargantuan Mi-26 transport helicopters the Russians were using was brought down on its approach to the airbase at Khankala. The overloaded helicopter from the 487th Separate Helicopter Regiment came down in the minefield around the base, resulting in 127 deaths.

However, such incidents were relatively infrequent, and with some 80,000 federal soldiers still present in-country and the Kremlin keeping a much tighter control of the media reporting on the war, nothing generated the kind of public and elite dismay as had been present during the First Chechen War. Furthermore, Putin moved quickly to re-establish the forms of constitutional order so as to give the appearance of normalization. In May, in a half-step forward, Moscow announced that it was taking over direct rule of Chechnya. This at least ended its previous ambiguous state of being a conflict zone essentially outside the regular laws of the state and was a prelude to establishing a local puppet government. In June 2000, Putin appointed Akhmad Kadyrov as the interim head of the Chechen government. Kadyrov was the most prominent of the former rebels who had defected to Moscow. The Chief Mufti of the ChRI, he was a prominent rebel during the First Chechen War but he was an outspoken critic of the Wahhabist jihadi school and this new generation regarded his moderate Islamic views with equal suspicion. In 1999, he and his son Ramzan broke with the ChRI and joined the federal side, bringing with him Kadyrov's personal militia. This force of *Kadyrovtsy* ('Kadyrovites') was to expand dramatically, not least as other deserters from the rebel cause flocked to join. After all, Kadyrov still retained considerable moral authority, paid well – and was known to ask no questions as to their previous activities.

OGV commanders in the Second Chechen War

1999	Colonel-General Viktor Kazantsev (Armed Forces)
2000	Colonel-General Gennady Troshev (Armed Forces)
2002	Colonel-General Valery Baranov (MVD)
2004	Colonel-General Yevgeny Baryayev (MVD)
2006	Major-General Yakov Nedobitko (MVD)
2008	Major-General Nikolai Sivak (MVD)

In another attempt to portray the conflict as all but over, or at least no more than a police action now, from 2002 successive OGV commanders came from the MVD VV, not the Armed Forces.

Assailed not just by federal forces but Chechen militias such as the *Kadyrovtsy*, the Yamadayevs' Vostok Battalion, as well as a separate Zapad (West) Battalion recruited by the GRU as a counterweight, the rebels were increasingly pushed onto the defensive and limited to small-scale raids and ambushes. They turned ever more to terrorist tactics and even suicide attacks (never previously a feature of Chechen guerrilla struggles). Controversially, this extended to terrorist attacks against Russian civilians, albeit probably without Maskhadov's approval. In October 2002, for example, some 40 terrorists seized the Dubrovka Theatre in Moscow, taking over 800 hostages. After two days of failed negotiations, a narcotic gas was pumped into the building, which was then stormed by the *Al'fa* counter-terrorist team. The terrorists were killed, but so too were 129 hostages, almost entirely because of adverse reactions to the gas. Later, in September 2004, another effort was made, when 32 jihadist terrorists seized School Number One in the North Ossetian town of Beslan on the first day of the new school year. Of the 1,100 hostages taken, most were children. On the third day of the ensuing siege, when one of the terrorists' bombs exploded, the building was stormed: 334 hostages died, including 186 children. However, while during the First Chechen War the authorities had been willing to compromise, under Putin the Kremlin took a tough line and continued its campaign to pacify Chechnya. If anything, he used it as the reason to intensify his efforts; after Beslan, he said: 'We showed weakness, and weak people are beaten.'

In March 2003, a new Chechen constitution was ratified by referendum, explicitly declaring the republic part of the Russian Federation, with Akhmad Kadyrov being formally sworn in as Chechen president later that year. While the rebels were down, they were not yet out, though. Attacks continued, most strikingly on 9 May 2004. Akhmad Kadyrov was receiving the salute at Grozny's Dinamo stadium during the annual Victory Day parade when a bomb exploded, killing him along with a dozen others.

Although his son Ramzan, who commanded the *Kadyrovtsy*, was too young formally to succeed him as

Left to right: General Gennady Troshev, Commander of the North Caucasus Military District, Defence Minister Igor Sergeyev, Chechen chief administrator Akhmad Kadyrov and mayor of Grozny Beslan Gantemirov pose for a picture after their talks in Grozny, November 2000. (REUTERS)

Terrorism was a key weapon of war. Here, in October 2017, flowers and candles have been placed in front of a memorial in memory of the victims of the Dubrovka theatre terrorist attack in Moscow, Russia. (dpa picture alliance / Alamy Stock Photo)

president – Interior Minister Alu Alkhanov was sworn in as a stopgap replacement – in effect he took over his father's role. In keeping with the rich Chechen tradition of the feud, he also redoubled his efforts to wipe out the remnants of the rebel movement. As it was, though, the rebel movement was already a shadow of its former self. Their leaders killed one by one, the rebel movement shrank and radicalized, with more and more nationalist guerrillas simply drifting quietly home when their hopes of a free Chechnya receded and their leaders increasingly seemed more interested in a greater holy war. Federal forces in-country were reduced to the newly formed 42nd Motor Rifle Division and MVD VV assets, but along with the *Kadyrovtsy* these were more than enough for the task. Meanwhile, the real focus of insurgency shifted to new conflicts elsewhere in the North Caucasus. Ingushetians, Dagestanis, Kabardins and other local peoples began challenging Moscow's rule and corrupt and ineffectual local governments, only to be crushed by a mix of tough security measures and the co-optation of local elites.

The Second Chechen War officially cost the Russians fewer than 7,500 dead: around 3,500 soldiers, 2,500 VV, 106 officers of the FSB and GRU and just over 1,000 Dagestani and Chechen loyalist 'militiamen.' That said, this may well understate the total losses, especially of local auxiliaries. Beyond that, they lost an estimated 45 helicopters (including 16 Mi-24 gunships) and eight fixed-wing aircraft (two Su-24 bombers and six Su-25 ground-attack aircraft), the latter more to accident and pilot error than rebel action. Likewise, the Kremlin's claims that rebel losses were 16,299 killed and 11,272 captured need to be taken with some caution, although they are probably not too far off the mark. Either way, the butcher's bill was eminently satisfactory for a Kremlin which wanted and needed a convincing victory, and which was not excessively concerned about the human cost. Putin had his defining political triumph, one that could demonstrate at home and abroad that Russia was, in his words, 'lifting itself off its knees'.

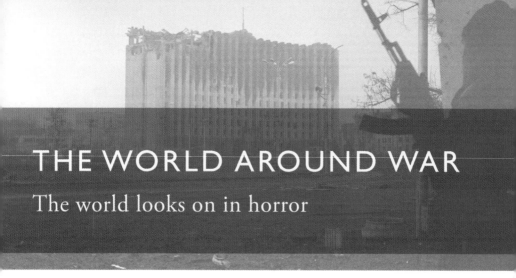

THE WORLD AROUND WAR
The world looks on in horror

We have strongly and consistently urged all sides to seek a political solution. A purely military solution is not possible. And so we urge Russia to take meaningful steps toward a political solution.
– US State Department spokesperson, December 1999

In an age when conflict has become a question of international law, media coverage and diplomacy, the two Chechen wars demonstrate both the limits of external constraints and the degree to which a still-powerful and above all determined nation can flout foreign opinion if it is willing to pay the price. Arguably, Moscow's willingness to invade Georgia in 2008, annex Ukraine's Crimean peninsula in 2014 and then invade the rest of the country in 2022 reflected the extent to which it was emboldened by the lack of meaningful international response to its tactics in Chechnya. Nevertheless, the conflict certainly had an impact on Russia's place in the world, not least in its short-lived rapprochement with the United States following the 9/11 attacks, when for one brief moment there seemed to be a common front against a common enemy.

Collateral damage
This was, after all, a war which was especially hard on the civilians caught in the middle, facing abuse,

displacement, and the ever-present danger of being caught in the crossfire, as illustrated by the tale of Ruslan Yusupov.* Born just outside Urus-Martan in 1965, although he heard all the tales of hardships the family had gone through in Kazakhstan, he himself had enjoyed a comfortable childhood: his father was an engineer, working for the local municipal government. He joined the Young Communist League for the social activities and because it helped him get into university; he studied medicine in Tbilisi, before returning to Chechnya to start work as a general practitioner in Grozny. He met and married Malika and they lived a relatively good life by Soviet standards; they had two sons, Kazbek and Musa, an apartment of their own, and a car, even if it was a battered Lada Niva.

When the Russians invaded in 1994, Ruslan volunteered for the ChRI forces, serving as a field medic during the first battle for Grozny. He was evacuated with some of the most wounded fighters to Shali to the south. A day later, while the fighting was still going on, he returned to Grozny to rejoin his family but discovered that a stray artillery round – almost certainly Russian – had hit his apartment block. His older son, Kazbek, was killed almost instantly.

He, Malika and Musa fled to Shali just as Grozny fell. For the rest of the war, Ruslan continued to practise medicine out of the ramshackle apartment they had managed to find, treating everyone from refugees to local officials. Occasionally, he was asked to treat some bearded young man with bullet wounds, no questions asked, and this he would do, before getting them out of his apartment as quickly as possible. A few times, Russian soldiers came to his apartment following tip-offs or rumours, but a combination of a poker face and judicious bribery sent them on their way.

---

* This is not his real name. He and his family were granted political asylum in the UK and I am using their story with permission but, in accordance with their wishes, I have changed their names and a few identifying details, as they still have relatives in Chechnya. I thank them for allowing me to draw on their experiences.

When the war ended, they returned to his home village outside Urus-Martan, but his family fell foul of the notorious and out-of-control Arbi Barayev, a local warlord-turned-crime boss. Ruslan never knew the details of the feud that had emerged between his family and Barayev, but one night in September 1997, the Yusupovs were visited by Ruslan's uncle, the village policeman and the local imam. It was explained to him that as part of this feud, they had heard that Barayev intended to kidnap them. Once again, they fled, moving to Gudermes.

Gudermes was one of the first towns taken as the Russians rolled back across the border at the end of 1999, after a short but bitter siege. Effective control of the city was precarious, with the Russians controlling the day and Chechens launching attacks by night. In mid-2000, with the introduction of more MVD VV and OMON personnel, the Russians began adopting a policy of widespread urban sweeps. Ruslan had the misfortune to be on the scene in October, when rebels made one of their rarer daylight attacks, a drive-by shooting on a patrol in a market. Russian forces quickly sealed the area and began arresting and beating Chechens, especially men, pretty indiscriminately. Ruslan arrested and taken to an army base.

He was one of over 100 Chechens detained in that sweep. Some were transferred to one of the infamous filtration camps; others were soon released. Ruslan, though, was interrogated repeatedly by Russian MVD officers – often suffering severe beatings – and then after two weeks transferred to the FSB's headquarters in the city. His FSB interrogator, a man he knew simply as Captain Bogdanov, would prove to be a one-man 'good cop/bad cop' routine, one minute offering him a drink and a cigarette, the next beating him savagely (he broke his left arm). Bogdanov's main aim seemed to be to try to force Ruslan to confess that he was a foreign agent stirring up rebellion.

Meanwhile, though, Malika had been able to speak to the newly installed Russian doctor heading Ruslan's

OPPOSITE
Civilians survived the siege of Grozny as best they could. Here, some women carry supplies into an improvised bunker as the Russian army begins its offensive on Grozny. (Photo by David Brauchli/ Sygma via Getty Images)

department at the hospital. Outraged by the situation, he apparently approached the local military authorities. Eventually a deal was brokered and Ruslan was released in return for a substantial bribe. Before he was released, though, he was forced to sign a document saying he had been co-operating with the authorities of his own free will. Bogdanov warned him that he ought to consider leaving Gudermes 'for his health'.

This Ruslan and his family did, ending up in the Satsita refugee camp in Ingushetia until forced to move back to Chechnya in 2003 as the authorities began to close it down. They returned to Urus-Martan (Barayev had been killed in 2001), but when the FSB began pressuring Ruslan to become an informant, threatening his surviving son, Musa, they fled Chechnya into Dagestan and then – thanks to Malika's family – were smuggled to the UK where they claimed and received asylum. As of writing, Ruslan is working as a hospital orderly and Malika as a cleaner. Musa, who missed much of his education, works occasionally as an unskilled labourer, but still suffers from panic attacks.

International condemnation

During the First Chechen War, the Russians tried to present themselves as fighting for order against gangsters and extremists, but this played rather poorly in the rest of the world. US President Bill Clinton warned Yeltsin that he risked feeding an 'endless cycle of violence' and human-rights organizations were especially outspoken in their criticisms. Human Rights Watch, for example, declared that 'Russian forces have shown utter contempt for civilian lives in the breakaway republic of Chechnya'.

The chaos and criminalization of Chechnya in the inter-war era did mean that, however opposed the international community might have been to Russian invasion and the methods used, Moscow could present itself as the guardian of order. The incursions into Dagestan had also demonstrated that Maskhadov either could not or would not restrain the jihadist commanders,

A Chechen digs a grave for a relative in Argun, after dozens of civilians were killed during a Russian bombing raid in January 1995. (Photo by David Brauchli via Getty Images)

and that this was a problem that could well grow. However, Moscow's attempts to present this as simply an 'anti-terrorist campaign' failed to win much sympathy in the West. During his presidential election campaign, US president-to-be George W. Bush warned in 1999 that 'even as we support Russian reforms, we cannot support Russian brutality'. Next year, speaking at the United Nations, US Secretary of State Madeleine Albright said that the Chechen conflict had 'greatly damaged Russia's international standing and is isolating Russia from the international community'.

Only China was supportive of Russia's position from the first, not least because it had its own concerns about separatists as well as an impatience with Western criticisms of its own human rights record. In 1999, for example, Beijing stated that 'the Chechen problem is clearly an internal affair of the Russian Federation and [China] supports the actions of the Russian government in fighting terrorist and separatist forces'. Next year, on a visit to Moscow, Chinese Defence Minister Chi Haotian went further, offering 'full support for the efforts which are being made by the Russian authorities in conducting the antiterrorist operation in Chechnya'.

Putin at US president George W. Bush's ranch for talks in November 2011. The Russian president believed that his support for the US 'Global War on Terror' after the 9/11 attacks would earn him indulgence for his methods in Chechnya. (Bob Daemmrich / Alamy Stock Photo)

The 9/11 card

However, the al-Qaeda 9/11 attacks in 2001 gave Moscow a perfect opportunity to reframe its campaign

as simply one more battlefield in a global struggle against extremist forms of Islam. Putin was among the first world leaders to contact President Bush to express his outrage at the attacks and to offer support. That day, he went on Russian television to hammer home the point:

> What happened today underlines once again the importance of Russia's proposals to unite the efforts of the international community in the fight against terrorism, against this plague of the 21st century ... Russia knows first-hand what terrorism is, so we understand more than anyone else the feelings of the American people.

He was as good as his word in supporting the US invasion of Afghanistan – even as many within the military elite smugly anticipated Washington finding itself sucked into the same morass that had greeted Moscow when the Soviets invaded in 1979 – and offering intelligence-sharing in the fight against international terrorists. All the same, this era of amity was not to last. With the 2001 US invasion of Afghanistan and the beginning of the campaign to shatter al-Qaeda as a coherent force, ironically enough that organization's ability to provide fighters and money to support the struggle in Chechnya rapidly dwindled. Furthermore, Washington began to lose patience with Moscow's attempts to caricature all the rebels as wild-eyed jihadists and its often-unsubtle manipulation of the intelligence it did share.

Ultimately, US–Russian relations would worsen, with Putin's efforts to retain control over the country and resist democratizing pressures, as well as his aggressive foreign policy, increasingly alarming Washington. Although a level of pragmatic intelligence sharing and co-operation continued, this was never as open and productive as originally hoped, as witness the intelligence gaps through which the Chechen Tsarnayev brothers – who bombed the Boston marathon in 2013 – slipped.

The Georgian factor

Just as Moscow was eager to present the Chechens as agents of international jihadist conspiracy, so too during a period of poor relations with neighbouring Georgia, the Russians were keen to paint Georgia as an ally of the rebels. It is certainly true that Georgia's Pankisi Gorge region, which abuts onto Chechnya, was used in the 1990s and 2000s by rebels as a refuge in which to rest and recover. This may have sometimes been with the knowledge and acquiescence of the Georgian government, but it is unclear how often this was the case. The Pankisi Gorge was a notoriously lawless region where the government's authority often counted for little and where two-thirds of the population were ethnic Kists, kin to the Chechens. Unsurprisingly, many Chechen refugees headed there, among whom was a minority of fighters. In August 2002, Russia bombed a village over the border and eventually the Georgians deployed over 1,000 troops into the Gorge to restore order and arrest

Georgian special forces soldiers on exercises in 2002, following Moscow's claims that Tbilisi was sheltering Chechen rebels in the Pankisi Gorge. (REUTERS/David Mdzinarishvili)

or expel fighters, as much as anything else to forestall any more extensive Russian response. After all, Russian defence minister Sergei Ivanov gave a heavy-handed hint referencing the US invasion of Afghanistan: 'The international community has just crushed the nest of international terrorism in Afghanistan … We must not forget about Georgia nearby, where a similar nest has recently begun to emerge.' Ultimately, Russo-Georgian relations would still lead to war, in 2008, but at least the pretext was not Chechnya.

Diasporas and brotherhoods

Especially during the First Chechen War, Moscow claimed not only that it was fighting to topple a criminal regime in Grozny but also that this regime was connected to and using the services of the wider Chechen criminal diaspora throughout Russia. In 1996, for example, Anatoly Kulikov claimed that strike teams of Chechen gangsters were being dispatched to cities across Russia, planning 'the complete destabilization of Russia'. This was a striking but also entirely fictitious claim. Indeed, while the Dudayev regime was thoroughly criminalized, there was actually a clear and widening division between the networks operating in Chechnya and those outside the republic. Nikolai Suleymanov, the powerful Chechen gangster known as 'Khoza', described this as the 'two Chechnyas'. While there were connections between the two, largely through kinship, in the main Russian-based gangs were very keen to limit their links with their counterparts in the homeland. In part, this was because they feared being targeted by the authorities as potential fifth columnists, but there was also a genuine cultural divide between those Chechens who were wheeling and dealing in a larger, predominantly Russian context and those who stayed locked within the tighter and smaller world of tradition and kin. In 1995, for example, Dudayev sent representatives to meet with kingpins in the *bratva* ('brotherhood') – a broad term to mean Chechen organized crime in Russia as a whole, not a specific

Akhmed Zakayev, prime minister of the rebel Chechen government in exile, holding a press conference in London, where he had been granted asylum. (Leon Neal/AFP via Getty Images)

gang – in the northern Russian town of Petrozavodsk. He hoped they would bankroll his regime, but not only did they refuse, they also, at a subsequent gathering in Moscow, banned direct transfers of money, men or weapons to the rebels.

This division only grew under Putin, when it was made very clear by the authorities that any hint of support for the rebels would bring savage reprisal. Given in any case that the *bratva* were unimpressed by the growing Islamic radicalism within the ChRI, they were even less inclined to help. Instead, they concentrated on their own pursuit of money and power in the Russian underworld. The irony was that where there were verified cases of organized crime factions selling weapons to the rebels, they were actually ethnic Russian gangs selling guns to Chechen rebels for them to shoot at fellow Russians.

On the other hand, there is a distinct ethnic Chechen diaspora outside Russia that did provide more support for the rebels. There are some 20,000 ethnic second-, third- or fourth-generation Chechens in Syria and 34,000 in Kazakhstan, but also a substantial diaspora in Turkey (where there may be up to 150,000) and across Europe. There has been a 'ChRI government in exile' in existence since 1999, as of writing presided over from asylum in the United Kingdom by moderate nationalist 'chairman of the council of ministers' Akhmad Zakayev, formerly Maskhadov's foreign minister. However, its actual influence is marginal. Indeed, in 2009, the jihadist Caucasus Emirate underground movement sentenced him to death on the grounds that he 'professes democratic religion, propagates secularism, and prefers the laws established by men to the Sharia law of Almighty and Great Allah.' Zakayev has outlived the Emirate, though. All the same, the Emirate and then the *Vilayat Kavkaz* local Islamic State franchise have been able to gain funds and material support from Turkish Chechens in particular, sometimes voluntarily and sometimes by extortion. A series of murders of prominent Chechens in Turkey accused of fundraising for the insurgency has been blamed on Moscow or Grozny, but this has not been proven.

HOW THE WAR ENDED
The end of the 'counterterrorist operation'

The leadership of Russia has officially confirmed the fact that the nest of terrorism has been crushed, that illegal armed groups have been neutralized, and militant leaders on whose conscience lay the grief and suffering of thousands of people have been destroyed, detained and brought to court.
– Ramzan Kadyrov, 2009

The Second Chechen War ended with a whimper rather than a bang. By March 2007, when Ramzan Kadyrov finally succeeded his father as Chechen president, large-scale combat operations had long since ended. Khattab, who had survived being blown up by a landmine and shot in the stomach with a heavy machine gun, had died in March 2002 when an FSB undercover agent passed him a letter that was steeped in poison. In February 2004 Yandarbiyev died in exile in Qatar, when a bomb blew up his car. The men convicted of his killing were eventually extradited to Russia – where they received a hero's welcome, apparently being GRU agents. In March 2005 Maskhadov, long since by then a general with no army, was killed by federal forces in Tolstoy-Yurt. Shamil Basayev was killed by a Russian booby trap in July 2006. Doku Umarov, who took up the poisoned chalice of titular head of the resistance movement in 2006, proved a lacklustre figure whose talents beyond staying alive were limited. In 2007, he declared the formation of the *Imarat Kavkaz* (IK; Caucasus Emirate), aiming to unite the nationalist and jihadist movements of the North Caucasus into a single common movement, but this never amounted to much on the ground. In 2013, even his capacity to survive was exhausted and he died in circumstances still unclear, but probably from Russian poison.

The rebel movement was increasingly dispersed, demoralized and divided. The Chechen population was exhausted by years of brutal war and draconian security measures. Ramzan Kadyrov's government, buttressed by his personal force of *Kadyrovtsy*, seemed to have the situation in hand. Thus, on 16 April 2009, the National Antiterrorism Committee of the Russian government issued a statement that the decree 'declaring a counterterrorist operation in the territory of the [Chechen] republic' was being repealed, so as to create 'the conditions for the future normalization of the situation in the republic, its reconstruction and development of its socio-economic sphere'. Through this banal press release, the Russian government in effect declared victory.

Russian forces in Chechnya had been reduced to around 10,000 soldiers, in the MVD VV's 46th Independent Special Designation Brigade and the Armed Forces' 42nd Motor Rifle Brigade. They were supported by the MVD VV's 34th Special Designation Detachment, a small counter-terrorist commando unit, as well as the MVD VV's 352nd Independent Reconnaissance Battalion and the MVD VV's 140th Artillery Regiment. The bulk of forces within Chechnya were Chechen MVD forces, built on the basis of the *Kadyrovtsy*: the 141st 'Akhmad Kadyrov' Special Purpose Police Regiment in Grozny, the 249th Independent Special Motorized VV Battalion 'Yug' (South) in Vedeno (formerly known as *Neftepolk*, the 'Oil Regiment'), the 424th Independent Special Designation Brigade and 359th Independent Special Police Motorized Battalion in Grozny and the 360th (Shelkovskaya), 743rd

The appeal hearings of Anatoly Bilashkov and Vassily Pokchov, convicted of the assassination of former Chechen president Zelimkhan Yandarbiyev in Doha. (KARIM JAAFAR/AFP via Getty Images)

(Vedeno) and 744th (Nozhay-Yurt) Independent VV battalions. While these technically were subordinated to the North Caucasus VV District headquarters in Rostov-on-Don in southern Russia (and later its successor agency, the National Guard), in practice it is widely acknowledged that their primary loyalty was likely to be to Grozny and Kadyrov.

By contrast, the rebels were down to no more than a few hundred fighters, largely stranded in the highlands, with perhaps 500 trying to integrate back into society, whether back with their families or hidden amid the population of displaced persons. In theory, they could have been considered sleepers, ready to return to the fray when the time was right, but in practice most appeared to be hoping or determined to turn their backs on the fight. Certainly by the late 2010s it seems that any who had not been captured, defected to the *Kadyrovtsy* or resumed anti-government activity had simply drifted back into civilian life.

Doku Umarov, who became leader of the remaining Chechen rebels in 2006 and self-proclaimed 'Emir

of the Caucasus Emirate' in 2007, did not prove to
be the kind of political leader with the charisma or
strategy to keep and enthuse them, and their numbers
fell every year. He fought in the First Chechen War,
initially under Ruslan Gelayev and then in his own unit,
which he called *Borz* ('Wolf'). He proved an effective
field commander and Maskhadov later appointed him
as head of the Chechen Security Council. One of his
primary roles in the inter-war period was trying to
resolve differences between factions and, especially,
the nationalists and the jihadists. Nevertheless, he was
dogged by allegations of involvement in the kidnap
'industry' – he came from the same *teip* as Arbi Barayev
– and was eventually forced to step down in 1999. This
appears to have embittered him, as from then on he
steadily drifted into the jihadist camp. He fought during
the siege of Grozny in 1999–2000, sustaining a head
wound and being evacuated from the city before it fell.
He continued to fight, but had by this time gravitated
towards Shamil Basayev's camp and also demonstrated
a willingness to launch and plan terrorist attacks. When
he became 'president of the ChRI' in 2006 following
the death of his predecessor, Adul-Khalim Sadulayev,
he made Basayev his vice president.

His proclamation of the IK reflected not just his own
jihadist view that the struggle in Chechnya was part
of a wider one to drive the Russians out of the North
Caucasus; it was also a product of the way that the
jamaats or insurgent groups outside Chechnya were even
by then more active and enthusiastic than his own. He
already had good links with the *jamaats* of Kabardino-
Balkaria and this was an attempt to try to use those
contacts to bolster his own authority and also bring the
various insurgent movements together. In that, it has
failed and the IK has no meaningful control over the
groups nominally under its umbrella.

Instead, Umarov had to turn to terrorism in a
bid to make an impact, not least when his authority
was under threat. Although he at times declared a
moratorium on civilian attacks, these tended to be

more propaganda than reality. In 2008, he revived the Al-Riyadus Martyrs' Brigade, a unit specifically tasked with recruiting and preparing suicide bombers. After all, the rebel campaign has become almost entirely one of terrorism. Furthermore, most of their 'spectaculars' took place outside Chechnya itself, such as the 2009

Loyalist Chechen special police on a raid on a suspected insurgent hideout in Grozny in July 2008. One would be killed in the lengthy firefight that ensued. (HASAN KAZIYEV/ AFP via Getty Images)

bombing of the Nevsky Express high-speed train from Moscow to St Petersburg, which killed 27 people, or the 2011 suicide bombing at Moscow's Domodedovo airport, which left 37 dead. These reflected the Chechens' ability to find a handful of willing bombers, as well as their links with other North Caucasus

In October 2010, insurgents killed four people in a suicide attack on the Chechen parliament. In the aftermath, women wash bloodstains off the adjacent road. (REUTERS/Kazbek Basayev)

jihadists. However, their operational capacities inside Chechnya itself had become severely limited. In August 2010, as much as anything else because of internal politics (facing a leadership challenge, Umarov needed to demonstrate that he could still act), insurgents launched a suicide operation against Kadyrov's home village of Tsentoroi. Two months later, three rebels launched a suicide attack on the Chechen parliament building in Grozny, killing two security guards and a parliamentary officer. On one level, these attacks were relatively ineffective, actually leading to more rebel casualties than among the security forces. Yet while their dependence on suicide tactics was a sign of the rebels' inability to penetrate the security cordons any other way, it was also evidence that they were, and likely still are, able to find people willing to die for the chance to strike a blow against the Kadyrov regime and his Russian backers.

Umarov himself was killed by the Russian FSB in 2013, reportedly by being poisoned, and his successor, the Dagestani Aliaskhab Kebekov, also known as Ali Abu Muhammad, was himself killed in a raid on his safehouse in April 2015. The third IK leader, Magomed Suleimanov ('Abu Usman Gimrinsky'), lasted only a month before being killed in an operation by the security forces, and so it was perhaps no wonder that the Emirate essentially self-destructed. Some of its members simply returned to civilian life, and the rest defected to *Vilayat Kavkaz* ('Caucasus Province'), the local incarnation of Islamic State, which was formed in 2015, and which continued to launch occasional and typically small-scale terrorist attacks.

CONCLUSION AND CONSEQUENCES
One war over, others just beginning

We are extremely satisfied. The modern Chechen republic is a peaceful and budding territory. The end of the counterterrorist operation will spur on economic growth in the republic.
– Ramzan Kadyrov, 2009

These were savage conflicts which combined at different times the characteristics of an imperial conquest, a civil war and a terrorist campaign. The impact on Chechnya itself was devastating: cities in rubble, populations fled into refugee camps, an economy shattered, communities torn apart by war and suspicion. To beat the rebels, Moscow created a new regime that international human rights organizations routinely describe as violent and dictatorial. Meanwhile, *jihad* and violent Islamic extremism entered the North Caucasus, while the struggle – and the propaganda that surrounded it – contributed to a climate of paranoia and xenophobia in the rest of Russia.

Chechnya reborn, Chechens recovering?
There still is no definitive figure for the number of civilian casualties from the two wars: anything from 70,000 to 200,000, out of a population of around 800,000 in

1989 (that census recorded a population of 1,277,000 for the Chechen-Ingush ASSR, and later accounts show Ingushetia having a population of around 450,000). At peak, the number of refugees reached perhaps another 400,000. Thus, of any 20 Chechens alive in 1989, by 2009, ten of them had experienced being a refugee at some point, and between two and five had died as a result of the war.

Since then, most refugees have returned home. Many of these displaced people have found work, thanks to massive injections of federal aid – in 2008, Moscow pledged $120 billion for the period to 2012 alone – not least in Ramzan Kadyrov's grandiose reconstruction projects. These range from building 'Europe's largest mosque' – if one considers Chechnya part of Europe – to an 80-storey 'vertical city' to be built in the capital's Grozny City-2 complex, both of which he named after his father. Nevertheless, around a third of the adult population remains unemployed and although central

The war led to a massive refugee problem. Here, displaced Chechen dismantle their tents in the Magas refugee camp in Ingushetia, as the Russians try to push them home to support their claims that the situation in Chechnya is 'normalising'. (Photo by Alexander Sorin/ Getty Images)

Grozny is now a glittering showcase city, many of the smaller towns and villages remain impoverished and unreconstructed.

A less visible but no less tangible effect of the war is the culture of suspicion, fear and recrimination that still lingers to this day. The campaign against the insurgents and those who sympathized with them – or were suspected of doing so – led to widespread abductions, disappearances and sweeps which saw young men in their dozens and hundreds sent to the infamous filtration camps, especially Chernokozovo, Titanic and the Pyatigorsk prison in the Stavropol Region. There they often faced torture, mistreatment and demands for bribes to be released. The non-governmental organization Human Rights Watch carried out an intensive investigation and reported:

Detainees arriving at Chernokozovo were met by two lines of baton-wielding guards forming a human gauntlet,

The Chechens did their best to mobilise global opinion to their cause. Here, their representatives join actress and activist Vanessa Redgrave and parliamentarian Ann Clwyd in calls for an international war crimes tribunal to examine allegations of abuses in Chechnya. (PA Images / Alamy Stock Photo)

and received a punishing beating before entering the facility ... [They were] beaten both during interrogation and during nighttime sessions when guards utterly ran amok. During interrogation, detainees were forced to crawl on the ground and were beaten so severely that some sustained broken ribs ... Some were also tortured with electric shocks.

Thousands of young Chechens disappeared during the wars, sometimes killed in the crossfire, sometimes murdered and their bodies dumped in mass graves. Those who survived often experience serious psychological trauma.

Kadyrov the king

Akhmad and more especially Ramzan Kadyrov have been crucial instruments of Putin's success in Chechnya. By installing a Chechen government – and two presidents who fought against the Russians in the First Chechen War – Moscow can claim a degree of legitimacy, even if international assessments are that the elections held to elevate both Kadyrovs were neither free nor fair. More to the point, by 'Chechenizing' the war and passing the bulk of the mopping-up operations to local forces, the Kremlin could minimize Russian casualties and get round the evident problems with the fitness, training and morale of many of its own troops. The *Kadyrovtsy* and similar Chechen forces, drawn largely from ex-rebels, knew the land and their enemies' tactics and hideouts. They also provided an escape valve, a means whereby rebels (and especially those of the old-school nationalist variety) who had tired of the struggle or who were disenchanted by the slide towards terrorism and jihadism could defect with safety and honour.

However, the irony is that in order to defeat the rebellion, the Kremlin may have granted Chechnya more autonomy in practice that it has had in the past two centuries. Kadyrov never fails loudly to proclaim his loyalty to President Putin. He also knows when to make good on that support. In the 2012 Russian presidential elections, for example, Chechnya reported an unparalleled 99.59 per cent turnout, with 99.82 per cent of voters backing Putin and 0.04 per cent for his next closest rival, the communist Gennady Zyuganov. If this were not dubious enough, one precinct even recorded a 107 per cent turnout. (The shine had come off by 2018, when Putin received a mere 91.44 per cent of the vote.)

At the same time, though, Kadyrov enjoys a level of freedom no other local leader in Russia enjoys. In part he has used that to eliminate precisely those agencies Moscow had hoped to use to balance and control him. That was, for example, one of the reasons why they kept the Yamadayevs and their Vostok Battalion outside Kadyrov's personal control. In 2003, though, Dzhabrail Yamadayev was killed by a bomb in his house; in 2008, Ruslan Yamadayev was shot dead in Moscow and the Vostok Battalion disbanded; the last Yamadayev brother, Sulim, fled to Dubai, where he was murdered in 2009. Likewise, he has dispatched assassins to kill his critics elsewhere in Russia and even in Europe, including his former bodyguard Umar Israilov, who had claimed that Kadyrov had personally tortured him (shot in Vienna, 2009) to doctor-turned-sniper Amina Okuyeva who joined the Ukrainian forces (killed in an ambush outside Kyiv, 2017).

Kadyrov also uses this autonomy to rule as an absolute and violent despot: the US State Department has noted 'compelling evidence that the government of Chechnya, under the control of Mr. Kadyrov, has committed and continues to commit such serious human rights violations and abuses as extrajudicial killing, torture, disappearances and rape'. Nevertheless, so long as he appears useful, then Moscow is willing to support, bankroll and protect Kadyrov. Around 80 per cent of the total Chechen budget is provided directly by the federal government. Indeed, given the extent to which he has brought the security forces under his own control and eliminated potential rivals, it is hard to see

Vladimir Putin, in 2011 during his proforma period as prime minister again but still the power behind the throne, meets his protégé, Chechnen leader Ramzan Kadyrov in Gudermes. (ALEXEI NIKOLSKY/AFP via Getty Images)

how the Kremlin could replace him without turning once again to force.

Fire in the Caucasus

The guerrilla war in Chechnya may be all but over, but the rest of the North Caucasus is periodically unstable, as a combination of unemployment, corruption and mismanagement sparks nationalist insurgencies that may use the rhetoric of Islam and formally be part of the Caucasus Emirate, but have on the whole not yet begun to follow the same jihadist path as the Chechens. This belies the initial triumphalism of many close to the Russian government. In 2005, Sergei Markov, director of the Russian Institute for Political Studies and a figure with close Kremlin ties, was talking up the success of the campaign: 'This war was a colossal success: the army of radical Islamists and separatists was crushed, peace and calm arrived. Americans and other countries should very carefully study the Chechen campaign carried out by the Kremlin and take lessons from it.' However, more sober observers were already looking at the spill-over effects. Former Ingush president Ruslan Aushev – a decorated veteran of the Soviet–Afghan War – warned that 'a huge cauldron is simmering there, in which there is Chechnya, and Dagestan, and Ingushetia, and Kabardino-Balkaria and Georgia, and each will be seeking its own interests'.

His words were more prophetic. Local terrorist and insurgent cells known as *jamaats* emerged across the region and proved less ambitious but far more active than the Chechens. They essentially focus on small-scale bomb and gun attacks on police, judges and officials,

Russian Interior Troops *Spetsnaz* storm a shop in Nalchik, capital of Kabardino-Balkaria, where gunmen had gone to ground after staging multiple attacks across the city in October 2005. (MAXIM MARMUR/AFP via Getty Images)

representatives of the state, although in a few cases they have united for major attacks. In October 2005, for example, some 200 militants from across the region attacked government buildings in Nalchik, the capital of Kabardino-Balkaria, and for two days virtually controlled the city before the security forces retook it. Such major attacks are rare, though, but still the centre of gravity of resistance to the Russians and their local governments has clearly shifted out of Chechnya, with Dagestan now experiencing the greatest violence. In 2010, for example, the Kabardino-Balkarian and Ingushetian *jamaats* killed roughly as many government police and troops as the Chechens, while the Dagestanis killed more than all three put together.

Umarov tried to unite the IK in the name of a global *jihad*. In October 2010, for example, he aligned himself with 'those mujahedin who are carrying out Jihad in Afghanistan, Pakistan, Kashmir and many, many other places'. While he described Russia as the 'most despicable' of them all, he placed the Chechen struggle in the context of a global war against 'the army of Iblis', the devil, combining 'the Americans, who today confess Christian Zionism, and European atheists, who do not confess any of the faiths'. This has, though, little traction among the *jamaats*; they are still motivated primarily by local practical and political concerns, not a vision of a global struggle.

Russia after Chechnya

The wars also had a serious impact on the rest of Russia. The official casualty figures for the first war were 5,700 federal police and soldiers dead, with a further 7,500 for the second, although these tallies have been questioned, not least as they may omit those dying of their wounds later in hospital. Beyond these figures, though, are the many less seriously wounded or those traumatized by what was an especially vicious and disturbing conflict, which saw atrocities committed by both sides. Beyond that, even though the public was more supportive of the

Second Chechen War, a fear of ending up being sent to Chechnya during either conflict was one of the factors behind massive levels of draft-dodging. In 2000 alone, following the invasion, it rose by 50 per cent. The wars also contributed to the rise of movements such as the Committee of Soldiers' Mothers, which campaigned to force the Kremlin to address issues of indiscipline, *dedovshchina* and the poor treatment of draftees, often with only limited success.

Indeed, the wars had a significant impact on the military as a whole. The First Chechen War in particular was a disaster in almost every respect. Looting, rape, murder and rampant crime were a constant factor (rebels would often re-arm themselves simply by buying guns from soldiers desperate for some food or drink). Morale hit rock bottom: some 540 NCOs and officers – including at least a dozen generals – resigned rather that serve in the war, or on receiving especially objectionable orders. Lieutenant-General Rokhlin, one of the few commanders to come out of the first battle of Grozny with any credit, refused the Hero of Russia medal – Russia's highest military honour – saying that he saw nothing glorious in fighting a war on his native soil. Although the Second Chechen War was less catastrophic, and allowed some units, especially the MVD VV and the VDV, the chance to build up some combat experience among their cadres of professional soldiers, it could not be said to have been a great boon, either. There is little public enthusiasm or sympathy for the veterans and the lacklustre performance of the Russian Armed Forces in the three-day war with Georgia in 2008 overshadowed the Russians' ability to beat the Chechens the second time round.

The conflicts also became something of a testing ground for the new Russian media. There were courageous journalists who risked their lives – and lost them – reporting on the realities of the realities on the ground. Anna Politkovskaya, an unflinching observer of the horrors meted out by both sides, was murdered in Moscow in 2006, in a killing widely believed to be because of her stand on Chechnya. On the other hand, an

awareness of the extent to which critical media coverage undermined public support for the First Chechen War meant that Putin made great efforts to control the story during the Second, putting further limitations on media already under considerable state pressure.

After all, there was one clear beneficiary. In 1904, Russian Interior Minister Vyacheslav von Plehve had advocated hostilities with Japan because 'a nice, victorious little war' was, he felt, just what Russia needed to regain its cohesion and self-esteem. Disaster in the Russo-Japanese War brought Tsarist Russia the 1905 Revolution, international contempt and bankruptcy.

Russian policemen at the site of a deadly bombing on a packed trolleybus in Volgograd on 30 December 2013, in which a suicide bomber killed 14 civilians. (STRINGER/AFP via Getty Images)

However, victory in the Second Chechen War was the making of Vladimir Putin, a perfect opportunity for a still-unknown figure to construct his image as the tough-talking and decisive defender of Russian national interests. From his early visits to the North Caucasus to be seen with the troops, to his street-slang references to the Chechens (in 1999 he memorably warned that 'if we catch them on the toilet, we'll whack them in the outhouse'), he used it masterfully to his political advantage. It may have led to widespread international condemnation, but domestically it allowed him to show a strong hand.

One price of this, though, has been a string of terrorist attacks in Russia. Mass attacks such as Dubrovka (2002) and Beslan (2004) have increasingly given way to suicide bombers. The most serious of these were bombings in Stavropol (2003), on the Moscow metro (2004) and two passenger airliners (2004), in the Moscow metro again (2010), at Domodedovo airport (2011) and in Volgograd (2013). Although these have not yet shaken Russia's resolve – if anything they have simply heightened traditional xenophobia towards people from the North Caucasus – they do reflect a continuing threat.

Kadyrov and the colonial wars

Part of the devil's bargain struck between Ramzan Kadyrov and Vladimir Putin was that Chechens could be called on when necessary in future wars. A company each from the Vostok and Zapad Special Battalions took part in the 2008 invasion of Georgia, while the former was still commanded by Sulim Yamadayev, although they were both disbanded shortly after. A Vostok Battalion was reconstituted in 2014, initially comprising Chechens and other 'mountaineers', to provide support to secessionists in the Donbas and project Moscow's authority, even though it was quickly 'Ukrainianised' with an influx of local recruits.

However, the main bulk of the *Kadyrovtsy* would remain within the Interior Troops and then, like the rest of the VV, were rolled into the new National Guard (the *Rosgvardiya*) when it was formed in 2016. It was clear that this was largely a formality, though, in that they reported to Kadyrov, not the new commander of the *Rosgvardiya*, General Viktor Zolotov. When committed to Ukraine during the 2022 invasion, for example, it quickly became clear that any orders from their notional field commanders from the regular army had to be approved by Grozny, contributing to repeated failures of coordination, and bad blood between the other forces and the Chechens.

Perhaps one of the more interesting uses of the *Kadyrovtsy* was in Russia's deployment to Syria, from 2015. In February 2015, opposition leader – and fierce Kadyrov critic – Boris Nemtsov was walking home across the Bolshoy Moskvoretsky Bridge in central Moscow when he was gunned down. It quickly emerged that the killers were Chechens, and even many within the Russian elite were in uproar about such a brazen act. Putin dropped out of sight as attempts were made to try and resolve the crisis, and eventually Kadyrov was forgiven, but part of the price was the deployment of *Kadyrovtsy*, wearing military police uniforms, to Syria from 2016. The idea was that they would better be able to interact with fellow Muslims – and, implicitly, that the wider Russian public would be less concerned with Chechen losses there.

Opposition politician Boris Nemtsov was a fierce critic of the war and of Ramzan Kadyrov. In February 2015, he was shot dead in central Moscow by a team of *Kadyrovtsy*, and here protesters express their anger at his murder. (Photo by Alexander Aksakov/ Getty Images)

Dreams of peace?
Is it too soon to talk about conclusions? After all, even if for this generation of Chechens the will and ability

to fight has largely been extinguished, Chechnya has been here before. If past experience is anything to go by, a future generation would be expected to pick up the struggle. This was certainly the assumption of General Kvashnin, architect of Russia's blundered first attack on Grozny and of its brutally effective second one. Speaking to prominent military journalist Pavel Felgenhauer in 1995, he said:

> We will beat the Chechens to pulp, so that the present generation will be too terrified to fight Russia again. Let Western observers come to Grozny and see what we have done to our own city, so that they shall know what may happen to their towns if they get rough with Russia. But you know, Pavel, in 20–30 years a new generation of Chechens that did not see the Russian army in action will grow up and they will again rebel, so we'll have to smash them down all over again.

Not only is it easy to believe that Chechnya cannot escape this vicious cycle, but it is also the case that while Chechnya may now largely be pacified, the rest of the North Caucasus is experiencing rising local nationalist and jihadist insurgency, which could yet blow back into Chechnya.

However, there are a few grounds for possibly thinking that Chechnya and Russia are not destined to stay in this spiral of rebellion and repression for ever. A new generation of Russians seems much less interested in being an imperial power, especially if that status proves costly, a lesson that may be reinforced by the experiences of war in Ukraine. In a 2013 poll, almost a quarter of Russians favoured independence for Chechnya, not so much out of sympathy for the region but because they were reluctant to see Russian blood and treasure spent on keeping it. One of the slogans of the anti-Putin opposition, after all, has been 'Stop Feeding the Caucasus', complaining about the money spent on subsidizing corrupt local regimes and maintaining substantial security forces there. They

Chechens in the Russo-Ukrainian War

When Vladimir Putin invaded Ukraine in February 2022, it was perhaps inevitable that Ramzan Kadyrov would jump on the opportunity to assert his martial credentials and his loyalty to Moscow. Indeed, Kadyrov and his men appear to have had more notice than most Russian officers. In an intercepted voice message he received from Lieutenant-Colonel Daniil Martynov, who was commanding the Chechen National Guard contingent there, he was told about the consternation – and dismay – of Martynov's fellow commanders when they were gathered in the week before the invasion to be told ('with bulging eyes') what was about to happen. Chechen special forces were reportedly deployed into Kyiv at the very start of the invasion in an abortive effort to assassinate Ukrainian president Volodymyr Zelensky. However, as it became clear that the invasion was not going

Chechen military volunteers from the Dzhokhar Dudayev Battalion preparing for a combat mission against Russian invaders in Ukraine in May 2023. The traditional Chechen wolf is juxtaposed with the *tryzub*, the Ukrainian trident symbol. (Photo by Yevhenii Zavhorodnii/Global Images Ukraine via Getty Images)

to be the anticipated walk-over, with the decimation of a company of Chechen National Guard, Kadyrov seems to have become unwilling to see them in the front line.

Although three units were deployed – the Akhmad Kadyrov Special Motorised Regiment, the 249th Separate Special Motorised National Guard Battalion Yug ('South'), and Special Battalion Vostok ('East') – the Chechens acquired something of a poor reputation amongst their peers as being, in the worlds of one disgruntled army officer, 'more interested in shooting videos for social media' and looting than actually fighting. Although Kadyrov claimed that Chechens had played a key role in a range of key engagements, including the siege of the fortified Azovstal steel in Mariupol, there is little evidence that they were often in the vanguard. Kadyrov even claimed to have joined front-line fighters in March 2022, although it later emerged that he had filmed his appearance from the safety of Grozny. He also used the war as an excuse to expand the *Kadyrovtsy*, raising four new 'Akhmat Battalions'. At least one was sent to Ukraine in autumn 2022, but as of writing there is no sign of a substantial Chechen role in the war.

Conversely, Chechens opposed to Kadyrov and the Kremlin had already been serving in the Ukrainian armed forces in the Dzhokhar Dudayev and Sheikh Mansur Battalions, and more flocked to the war in 2022. Two new units were formed: the Separate Special Purpose Battalion within the Ukrainian Foreign Legion and the rather smaller Khamzat Gelayev Joint Task Detachment. None of these units are anywhere near full battalion strength, but nonetheless they have proven rather more aggressive and enthusiastic fighters than Kadyrov's men.

might sympathize with the words General Mikhail Orlov wrote in 1820:

> It is just as hard to subjugate the Chechens and other peoples of this region as to level the Caucasian range. This is not something to achieve with bayonets but rather with time and enlightenment, in such short supply in our country. The fighting may bring great personal benefits to Yermolov, but none whatsoever to Russia.

It is true that a few Russians did gain from the almost two decades of war, but many more suffered. Likewise, though, while the Chechens are unlikely to be beaten into submission, in the future they may themselves look to something other than armed insurrection. After all, Chechens are changing. In many ways the resurgence of the traditions of *teip* and *adat* in the late 1980s and early 1990s was a short-lived phenomenon, as Chechens reacted to the collapse of the Soviet order by turning to the past to find a new identity. But not only did this sit uncomfortably with the rise of jihadist Islam; it is also an increasing anachronism in an age when Chechens are beginning once again to travel, to see other cultures,

ТРЕБУЕМ
ПРИЗНАНИЯ ГОС.
НЕЗАВИСИМОСТИ
ИЧКЕРИИ!

A protester holds a placard reading 'we demand the acknowledgement of the independence of the state of Chechnya' in December 1999, but the pressure for Chechen independence has largely subsided since, crushed between the Kremlin and Kadyrov. (REUTERS)

to go to university, to embrace modernity. Looking beyond Kadyrov, there is no reason why the Chechens could not take advantage of the autonomy he has carved out within the Russian Federation and build for themselves the kind of country they want to see – and to be able to do so without another round of murderous war and rebellion.

CHRONOLOGY

1585	Ottoman Empire claims control over Chechnya.
1722–23	Russo-Persian War pits Safavid Iran against Peter the Great's Russia.
1783	Treaty of Georgievsk implicitly cedes North Caucasus to Russian Empire
1784	Sheikh Mansur leads first rebellion against Russians.
1785	Russian defeat at the battle of the Sunja River.
1817–64	Caucasus War.
1818	Russians found fort of Groznaya; later becomes city of Grozny.
1834–59	Imam Shamil's revolt against the Russians.
1859	Chechnya formally annexed to Russian Empire.
1862	Chechnya formally subjugated.
1877–78	Chechen revolt crushed.
1917	Chechnya joins Union of the Peoples of the North Caucasus.
1918	Following collapse of Tsarist Russia, Union of the Peoples of the North Caucasus declares independence.
1918–22	Russian Civil War.
1920	Bolsheviks occupy North Caucasus.
1921	Mountaineer Autonomous Soviet Socialist Republic formed.
1924	Mountaineer Autonomous Soviet Socialist Republic divided into constituent regions and republics.
1934	Chechen-Ingush Autonomous Region formed.
1936	Chechen-Ingush Autonomous Soviet Socialist Republic formed.
1944	Stalin orders deportation of Chechen population.
1956	Chechens begin to be allowed home.
1991	**October** Presidential elections held in Chechnya, won by Dzhokhar Dudayev; he declares independence.
	November Russian President Yeltsin refuses to acknowledge Chechen independence.

1992   **March** Constituent elements of Russian Federation sign a new federation treaty bar Chechnya and Tatarstan.
June Split of republics of Ingushetia and Chechnya recognized by Moscow. Chechnya declares itself an independent state. Moscow refuses to accept this.
December Ingushetia breaks away to become a separate republic within the Russian Federation.

1994   **November** The Russian-backed Provisional Chechen Council launches abortive coup.
December Russian forces invade Chechnya 'to restore constitutional order'.

1995   **May** Chechen fighters seize hundreds of hostages at Budyonnovsk hospital, forcing Russian prime minister Viktor Chernomyrdin into negotiations.
July Ceasefire agreed.
December Ceasefire falls apart.

1996   **April** Dudayev is killed by Russian missile; he is succeeded by Zelimkhan Yandarbiyev.
August Chechen rebels retake Grozny. Khasav-Yurt Accord signed.
November Peace settlement agreed; end of the First Chechen War.

1997   **January** Aslan Maskhadov wins Chechen presidential elections; recognized by Moscow.
May Yeltsin and Maskhadov sign peace accords.

1998   **December** Four engineers from Britain and New Zealand are kidnapped and beheaded.

1999   **August** Chechen extremists launch cross-border attack into Dagestan. Vladimir Putin appointed Russian prime minister.
September Moscow blames Chechen rebels for a series of apartment bombings.
October Russian forces move into Chechnya.
December Putin replaces Yeltsin as acting Russian president.

2000   **February** Russian forces take Grozny.
March Putin wins Russian presidential election.
May Russia announces direct rule of Chechnya.
June Akhmad Kadyrov appointed head of Russian-backed government in Grozny.

2002	**October** Chechen terrorists seize the Dubrovka theatre in Moscow, holding over 800 people hostage; 129 hostages die when Russian forces use gas when storming the building.
2003	**March** New Chechen constitution is ratified.
2004	**May** A suicide bomber kills Akhmad Kadyrov. **September** Terrorists seize school in Beslan, southern Russia; more than 300 are killed when it is stormed.
2005	**March** Rebel president Maskhadov is killed.
2006	**March** Ramzan Kadyrov becomes Chechen prime minister.
2007	**March** Ramzan Kadyrov appointed Chechen president. **October** Doku Umarov declares the Caucasus Emirate.
2009	**April** Kremlin declares 'counter- terrorism operation' in Chechnya over. End of the Second Chechen War.

FURTHER READING

Akhmadov, I. & Lanskoy, M. *The Chechen Struggle: Independence Won and Lost* (Palgrave, 2010)

Babchenko, A. *One Soldier's War* (Grove, 2007)

Baiev, K. *The Oath: a surgeon under fire* (Walker & Co., 2004)

Billingsley, D. *Fangs of the Lone Wolf: Chechen Tactics in the Russian-Chechen War 1994– 2009* (Helion, 2013)

Bunich, I. *Khronika Chechenskoi voini* [Chronicle of the Chechen war] (Oblik Press, 1995)

Dunlop, J. *Russia Confronts Chechnya* (Cambridge University Press, 1998)

Eldin, M. *The Sky Wept Fire: My Life as a Chechen Freedom Fighter* (Portobello, 2013)

Felgenhauer, P. 'Degradation of the Russian Military: General Anatoli Kvashnin', ISCIP *Perspective* 15, 1 (October–November 2004)

Galeotti, M. '"Brotherhoods" and "Associates": Chechen networks of crime and resistance', *Low Intensity Conflict & Law Enforcement* 11 (2002)

Galeotti, M. *Russian Paramilitary and Security Forces since 1991* (Osprey, 2013)

Glenn, R. (ed.) *Capital Preservation: Preparing for Urban Operations in the Twenty-First Century* (RAND Corporation, 2001)

Goltz, T. *Chechnya Diary* (Thomas Dunne, 2003)

Grodnenskii, N. *Pervaya Chechenskaya* [First Chechen] (FUAiform, 2007)

Human Rights Watch. *Welcome to Hell: arbitrary detention, torture and extortion in Chechnya* (HRW, 2000)

Jagielski, W. *Towers of Stone: The Battle of Wills in Chechnya* (Seven Stories, 2009)

Kulikov, A. & Lembik, S. *Chechenskii Uzel: khronika vooruzhennogo konflikta 1994–1996 gg* [Chechen Knot: chronicle of the armed conflict 1994–1996] (Dom Pedagogiki, 2000)

Lieven, A. *Chechnya. Tombstone of Russian Power* (Yale University Press, 1998)

Mladenov, A. *Mil Mi-24 Hind Gunship* (Osprey, 2010).

Mladenov, A. *Sukhoi Su-25 Frogfoot* (Osprey, 2013)

Oliker, O. *Russia's Chechen Wars, 1994–2000* (RAND Corporation, 2001)

Politkovskaya, A. *A Dirty War* (Harvill Press, 2001)

Politkovskaya, A. *A Small Corner of Hell: Dispatches from Chechnya* (University of Chicago Press, 2007)

Sakwa, R. (ed.) *Chechnya: from past to future* (Anthem, 2005)

Schaefer, R. *The Insurgency in Chechnya and the North Caucasus: From Gazavat to Jihad* (Praeger, 2011)

Seely, R. *The Russian-Chechen Conflict 1800–2000: A Deadly Embrace* (Routledge, 2001)

Smith, S. *Allah's Mountains* (Tauris, 1998)

Tishkov, V. *Chechnya: Life in a War-Torn Society* (University of California Press, 2004)

Vatchagaev, M. *Chechnya: The Inside Story* (Open Books, 2019)

Wilhelmsen, J. *Russia's Securitization of Chechnya: How War Became Acceptable* (Routledge, 2016)

INDEX